The Paradise Island Story

Paul Albury

Second Edition

Revised by
Anne and Jim Lawlor

MACMILLAN
CARIBBEAN

Macmillan Education
Between Towns Road, Oxford OX4 3PP
A division of Macmillan Publishers Limited
Companies and representatives throughout the world

www.macmillan-caribbean.com

ISBN 1 4050 0243 3

First published 1984
Second edition published 2004

Designed by Gary Fielder at AC Design
Illustrated by Martin Sanders
Cover design by Gary Fielder at AC Design
Cover photograph by Kerzner International

Printed and bound in Thailand

2008 2007 2006 2005 2004
10 9 8 7 6 5 4 3 2 1

Contents

Foreword

Dr David Livingstone resides at the Ocean Club not because he explored The Bahamas as he did the African continent, but because the first contemporary visionary of Paradise Island, Huntington Hartford, the A & P heir, an ardent admirer of Livingstone, acquired and placed a large bronze statue of Livingstone in the Versailles Garden.

Dr Livingstone lived for 60 years, 1813–1873, and in his mature years uttered words of lasting value: 'If success attend me, grant me humility. If failure, resignation to thy Will.'

And so, this little known mantra has in so many ways prophetically touched all those who came to create in Paradise Island the fantasy of the ultimate experience of the 'get away' from the drudgery of everyday existence.

The story of Paradise Island does not attempt to make a historical assessment of Huntington Hartford, James M Crosby, I G 'Jack' Davis, Donald Trump, Merv Griffin or Sol Kerzner. What we have is a journey of magical proportions through time and a series of financial adventures and escapades. For this writer who lived up close through each period, the journey was incredulous and wonderfully stimulating. But for one exception, the dreams and visions of those men who had a special attachment to Paradise Island in the end became markers in a desolate field of memories.

And then Sol Kerzner – a man of single-minded vision, who came, who saw and who created reality from fantasy. The transformation, as if planned by destiny decades ago, made Paradise Island the hemisphere's complete 'wonderland' for the discerning and maybe not so discerning traveller. The strong artistry expressed in the architecture and the feeling of a lost empire casts a spell over those who venture in. It is believed that each night Atlantis and Paradise Island are showered with pixie dust, which makes each morning's awakening a euphoric occurrence.

The appeal, the charm and the magnetism of Paradise Island are unquestioned. One can understand how Nicholas Trott must have felt as he looked across the harbour in the late seventeenth century and absorbed the natural beauty of what then was known as 'the Long Island that maketh the harbour'. He knew that the island had to be his and as Governor he had the connections to make that happen.

We know the distant past, we understand and have lived the recent past, we appreciate the present and, as for the future, let's just say that the best is yet to come.

In capturing the colourful history of Paradise Island, Dr Paul Albury wrote with a charm and simplicity that made the story so alive. In keeping with that spirit and style, Jim and Anne (Paul's daughter) Lawlor continued Paul's work. The Paradise Island Story is now in the present.

J Barrie Farrington

Ocean Club Golf Course and Club House.

Dedication to First Edition

To my wife Joan
who endured to the end

Dedication to Second Edition

To Joan, Lisa and Liz
for their loving support

Acknowledgements

First Edition:
Among those who have helped me, in one way or another, I owe special thanks to the following: the staffs of the Department of Archives, and the Nassau Public Library; Mrs Doris Bullard, *The Tribune;* Miss Ethelyn Thompson, *Nassau Guardian;* Messrs Edward Bode and D Lester Brown; Pilot Frederick Brown; Miss Antonina Canzoneri; Mr & Mrs John Dahllof; Messrs Barrie Farrington & Charles Hall, Sr; Mrs Mae Higgs; Mr Anthony Hing-Cheong; Ms Rhoda Ireland; Mr Geoffrey A D Johnstone; Messrs Berdelle Key, Jim Lawlor & Roy MacKeen; Sir Asa Pritchard; Dr George C Rogers, Jr; Messrs Barry Scott & Bruce Smith; Mrs Betty Smith; Mrs Elizabeth Smith; Mr Andrew Toogood.

Above all, I am grateful to my daughter, Anne Lawlor, whose untiring research and dedication made the book possible.

Second Edition:
Special thanks to Ed Fields, Sandra Eneas, Cindi Scavella, Barrie Farrington, Sol Kerzner, Matt Knowles, Jackson Burnside, Jim Boocher, Dan Stevens, Pat Paul, the staff of the Department of Archives, Andrea Brownrigg, Marsha Saunders, Marva Dorsett, Ron Lightbourn, Orjan Lindroth, Roberta Ivano, Ashley McBain, Andrew Aitken, Michael Toogood, Etienne Dupuch Publications.

The author and publishers wish to acknowledge the following photographic sources:
Andrew Aitken pp. 88, 89, 90, 91 (top); Paul Albury Collection pp. 20, 28 (bottom), 30, 39 (bottom), 40, 42, 46, 47 (top and bottom), 70 (bottom), 78 (left), 84; Bahamas Historical Society p. 44; Bahamas Ministry of Tourism pp. 50-51; Bahamas Tourist News Bureau p. 70 (top); Lady Virginia Christie pp. 22, 27; Department of Archives pp. 1, 2, 3, 8, 16, 21, 25 (left), 26 (top and bottom); Monroe Dreher p. 25 (right); Etienne Dupuch, Jr. Publications pp. 58 (left), 60 (right); Peter Earle pp. 5, 6, 7, 9, 10 (left and right); Freud Communications/ Kerzner International pp. 95, 125; Paul Harding pp. 100, 102 (middle left), 105 (top), 121 (bottom); Kerzner International pp. v, 68, 69, 97 (all), 98 (top and bottom), 101 (top and bottom) 102 (top and middle right) 108 (bottom), 111 (top), 115 (top), 119 (bottom), 122, 124, front cover; Jim Lawlor pp. 39 (top), 54, 55, 62 (bottom), 91 (bottom), 102 (top left), 104, 105 (bottom), 110 (left and right), 114 (top left), 120-121 (top); Ron Lightbourn pp. 45, 49, 61 (bottom); Orjan Lindroth pp. 57, 59, 60 (left and right), 61 (top), 62 (top), 67; National Galleries of Scotland p. 28 (top); Resorts International (Bahamas) Ltd. pp. 73 (left and right), 75 (all), 76, 77, 78 (right), 80, 81 (top and bottom), 82 (left and right), 83, 85, 87; Robert Ranson p. 38; Gus Roberts p.94; Roland Rose p.123; Neil Sealey p 99 (top); Sarah Smith pp. 102 (bottom),103, 106 (top and bottom), 107, 108 (top), 109, 111 (bottom), 112, 113 (all), 114 (bottom left and right), 115 (bottom), 116, 117 (all) 118, 119 (top); Lady Margaret Symonette p. 41 (top and bottom); Andrew Toogood pp. 13, 18, 58 (right); Michael Toogood p. 124 (image inside raindrop Jim Lawlor); *The Tribune* pp. 35 and back cover (Ron Lightbourn), 65

Maps are based on maps from the Department of Lands and Surveys, Nassau and the Public Record Office, London. Map of Paradise Island Colony Subdivision (p. 79) is based on a map by Jim Lawlor. Map of Kerzner properties (p. 102) is based on a map by James Noel Smith.

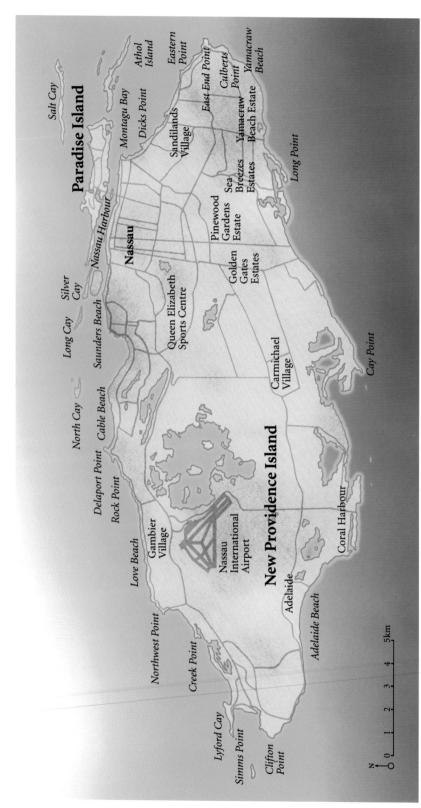

Paradise Island.

1
Discovery and Proprietary Government

*P*aradise Island lies close to the north shore of New Providence, being separated from its *larger neighbour by only a few hundred yards. The channel running between the two disparate islands is the historic harbour of Nassau. In the sense of the development of a community, Paradise was never settled. Rather, over the centuries it has performed the role of an adjunct to the capital island.*

It would be interesting to know the date and circumstances of the first ship to enter Nassau harbour. But since that information is not presently known to us, we have to be content with some general hypotheses.

A frenzy of Spanish maritime activity followed Columbus's epochal first voyage of discovery in 1492. In communicating with their American possessions, sea captains of Spain often found it convenient to sail near, or through, The Bahamas. In the process they explored many of our islands to take on supplies of salt, firewood and water, and to search for any product that might prove commercially valuable.

In 1651 a book entitled *A Description of the New World* was published. Its author, George Gardyner, claimed that the islands were, at the time of writing, uninhabited and that, although little known to the English seamen who sailed around them yearly, they were visited frequently by the Spaniards who obtained sarsaparilla, sassafras, ambergris and other products from them.[1]

If, as Gardyner says, the Spaniards were frequent visitors to the archipelago, it is unlikely that New Providence, Paradise Island and the fine harbour they embrace would have escaped their notice. However, the date of the author's writing must have been some years before the time of publication, for The Bahamas was indeed inhabited by 1651. In fact, the island of Eleuthera had been settled by the Eleutheran Adventurers some three years before that.[2] And, in this respect, we have to consider the Bermudians.

Bermuda was settled in 1612. The pioneer English colonists found the islands uninhabited, except by numerous wild hogs, and covered with forests of beautiful cedar trees. The hogs helped to keep this band alive and the cedar was found to be excellent timber for the building of houses and ships. The colonists quickly gained experience in voyages to the mainland colonies and soon thereafter were combing the Bahamas chain in search of Spanish wrecks and ambergris.

As a territory of England, The Bahamas Islands were granted, in 1629, to Sir Robert Heath, Attorney General of England, who was unable to fulfil the conditions of the grant that he create a settlement in The Bahamas.

By the mid 1640s, however, Bermudian sea captains were scrutinising the archipelago for more compelling reasons. A number of their countrymen had decided to leave their homeland because of religious persecution and several vessels were sent to The Bahamas to find a suitable island for their new abode.[3] Subsequent history suggests that these explorers had selected Eleuthera. Yet, as in the case of the Spaniards, it is difficult to believe that during, or even before, their intensive search they had not discovered New Providence.

Rightly or wrongly the mantle of 'discovery' was to fall on the shoulders of Captain William Sayle, leader of the Eleutheran colonists, and himself a Bermudian. And the event of discovery seems to have taken place some few years after the Eleutheran settlements were established. According to one account, Sayle was on a voyage to Carolina when his ship met with a storm and was driven this way. He found refuge in the harbour and was preserved from shipwreck. Sensing divine guidance he named the island Providence.[4]

Another account does not mention Sayle's near escape and discovery, but states that the island, when first settled, was known as Sayle's Island. The first people to go there were very poor and their transportation was paid by the more prosperous members amongst their religious persuasion. Seeing the hand of God in their deliverance from persecution they called their new home Providence.[5]

However true this might have been, we do know that in 1666, some 18 years after the first band of colonists landed at Eleuthera, another group of Bermudians settled New Providence. Unlike the Eleutherans these new settlers seem to have prospered from the very beginning and by 1670 their number had increased to 300.[6]

The Puritan Eleutheran Adventurers had instituted a form of government which they styled a 'Republic.' There is no doubt that they thought their grant of all the Bahama Islands, authorised by Parliament, to be secure. But, of course, those were the heady days of religious, political and military conflict in England when Oliver Cromwell ruled the roost. Charles I had been beheaded in 1649 and the monarchy was not restored until 1660.

Charles II did not have much use for Puritans,

The Eleutheran Adventurers – Shipwreck on North Eleuthera, 1648.

Republics or Acts of Cromwell's Parliament and, consequently, the claim of the Adventurers to The Bahamas was not sustained. Nevertheless, it was necessary that the islands be granted to some body which would be entrusted with the task of instituting a government and promoting the development of the islands. The body which received the onerous distinction was composed of six men who were close friends of the King and already the Proprietors of Carolina. They are known in history as the Lords Proprietors of The Bahamas.

The advent of proprietary government brought about two important changes: the Republic of Eleuthera came to an end and the seat of government was established in New Providence. Thus, Paradise Island suddenly became a part of the centre of Bahamian life and activity.

At this stage it should be pointed out that Paradise is a relatively new name which has been used at this stage in our story only to ensure proper identification. Now that that objective has been accomplished we shall, in future, use the name that is contemporary with the period of discussion – for names too have a story to tell.

The settlement which developed on the north shore of New Providence was called Charles Towne in honour of Charles II who then sat on the English throne. The townspeople, and especially the seafaring among them, recognised the paramount importance of the nearby island in providing them with a splendid harbour.

In a sense it seems remarkable that they did not bestow a name on that island which lay before their eyes every day. But it seems that they were content in identifying it by a geographical description: 'the island which makes the harbour' or 'the island which forms the harbour'. It was not until the end of the seventeenth century that it was given a name of its own. Therefore, until we arrive at that time in our story, we shall refer to it simply as 'the island'.

It must be remembered that during the boisterous, early history of the area, Charles Towne, New Providence, was the centre of activity and the island, for the most part, played the role of a placid satellite. Nevertheless, it is necessary to have an understanding of that early history so as to see the island in its proper perspective.

The seafaring settlers of Charles Towne were a stubborn and intractable lot. They had been accustomed to gathering wreck-goods, ambergris, salt and hardwood and disposing of these goods to their best advantage, unhindered by controls and taxes. Thus, the establishment of a government was seen by them as an interference in their free way of life, an interference to which they reacted at the slightest provocation.

King Charles II (1660–1685) granted rights to The Bahamas to the Lord Proprietors from South Carolina, and began the first positive effort at settling the islands by creating the town of Nassau, previously known as Charles Towne, and the first fort, Fort Nassau, between 1695 and 1697.

According to the constitution, governors were to be appointed by the Proprietors. Notwithstanding this, the people elected their own first governor, John Wentworth, although they knew very well that the Proprietors had decided to appoint his brother, Hugh, to the post. The problem was solved when Hugh conveniently died and the Proprietors agreed to let John remain as Commander-in-Chief.[7]

One man who was not pleased with this inauspicious start was John Darrell. He had played an important part in settling New Providence and he did not think much of John Wentworth as Governor. 'Captain John Wentworth,' he wrote, 'debauches himself and has corrupted the people to drink. They have chosen him governor and neglect their crops.' Darrell further complained that the young men were averse to hard work, preferring to 'run a-coasting in shallops, which is a lazy course of life'.[8] Wentworth seemed to be much to the liking of the people in general but the Proprietors were inclined to believe that he was lax in taking care of their interests. After all, they had each invested £200 in

The Bahamas and the returns thus far were next to nothing.

After about five years of service they let Wentworth go and replaced him with Charles Chillingworth. Oldmixon, who wrote the earliest English history of The Bahamas, stated that the inhabitants 'living a lewd licentious sort of life... were impatient under Government. Mr Chillingworth could not bring them to reason: They assembled tumultuously, seized him, shipped him off for Jamaica, and lived every Man as he thought best for his pleasure and interest.'[9]

Chillingworth's successor, Robert Clark, took office in 1677 and he soon became embroiled in a mini-war with the Spaniards. According to his story, Spanish ships made a number of incursions in Bahamian waters, seizing vessels, committing robberies and taking away farmers as prisoners, to be lodged in the dungeon of Havana.[10] In reprisal, Clark commissioned privateers and sent them out to plunder and destroy Spanish ships. Havana responded with howls of protest and English officials were incensed that a petty governor was endangering the peace in such a manner.

Clark was fired and Richard Lilburne sent out to replace him. But by this time, the Spanish had reached the end of their patience and were determined to destroy the privateering base of Charles Towne once and for all. Lilburne had only been in Charles Towne a few days when he was awakened one morning by the noise of cannon fire. The Spaniards had struck and before he could sound the alarm Government House had been taken. Lilburne saved himself by fleeing his house and hiding in the woods.[11] Clark, who was still in town, was not so lucky. Him the Spaniards captured, clapped in chains and took away with them when they left. He was subsequently killed and it is reported that his body was afterwards roasted on a spit.[12]

The Spaniards did much damage, pillaging Charles Towne to the extent of £20,000. They took some of the inhabitants prisoner and left the same afternoon. Later in the year, they returned to do a more thorough job. On this second occasion, 15 November 1684, the town was pillaged again and, except for a few buildings, was burnt to the ground.[13]

As we have seen, the first 14 years of proprietary government were unsettled times for New Providence. The last years of that period, when Charles Towne was wiped from the map, were far worse than the beginning. By that time, the Proprietors must have despaired of ever making a penny out of their troublesome grant. One of their number, however, the second Duke of Albemarle, was to receive a bonanza larger than he had ever expected to see from these parts, and from a source of which he never dreamed. The first duke had been largely responsible for the restoration of Charles II and because of that he was, as we say, in royal favour. No doubt the King was pleased to reward him by including him among the grantees of Carolina and The Bahamas. In London, on a day in March 1686, the second Duke of Albemarle met with a rugged Boston sea captain who told him of a galleon-load of silver which lay at the bottom of the Bahama Sea, there for the taking.[14]

2
Sir William Phips

*W*illiam Phips was born in 1650 on a plantation in Maine, New England. Having a predilection for the nautical world, at the age of 18 years he moved to Boston where he apprenticed himself to a shipbuilder. After a few years at this trade, he married a merchant's widow of some means and was able to establish his own shipyard. He built a vessel for himself, engaged first in the coastal lumber trade and thereafter began voyaging to The Bahamas and the West Indies.

We suspect that it was in New Providence harbour that Phips first heard about Spanish wrecks in Bahamian waters. Thoughts of gold and silver at the bottom of the sea excited his adventurous spirit, as well as his longing for wealth and fame, and he soon joined the growing band of treasure hunters.

His first adventure of this kind was to a wreck described as being 'near New Providence'. When he arrived at the site he found it swarming with vessels and divers, for seamen were attracted to Spanish wrecks as flies to carrion. Most of the readily accessible silver had already been retrieved. Phips, however, had a determined spirit and by employing the best diving gear he could obtain, did manage to salvage some bullion, but hardly sufficient to defray the expenses of the voyage.

Coral diving in the Mediterranean, thought to be similar to diving operations in the Caribbean.

A diving bell.

that way gave the banks a wide berth, but despite the hazards Phips was anxious to be upon them and in search of the sunken galleon.

He first tried to raise money for the venture in the Boston area. But the tight-fisted New England financiers showed no interest in tales of treasure somewhere on the sea-bottom. Phips then decided on a bold course of action: he would go straight to the King of England. From our time and place it might seem a little farfetched that the King would be interested in Bahamian treasure hunting, but Charles II was an inveterate gambler who was not easily 'fazed by a long shot'. Furthermore, because of his profligate life-style, he was chronically short of money and the possibility of coming into possession of a few tons of silver was an exciting thought.

The wreck of the Spanish galleon which occupied Phips's thoughts is, in itself, a fascinating story, but in this account it will have to be severely capsulised.

In 1641 a Spanish silver fleet was on the homeward voyage when it met with a hurricane between the American mainland and Bermuda. After the storm abated, the crew of one of the ships, the *Concepción*, looked about the watery waste and saw that the rest of the fleet had either scattered out of sight or gone down. The *Concepción* herself, heavily laden with treasure, was waterlogged and her sails had been blown away.

With almost superhuman efforts, the ship was pumped dry and its leaks stopped. Jury sails were rigged and the captain decided to make for Puerto Rico and a Spanish shipyard where essential repairs could be effected.

The *Concepción*, however, was destined never to reach Puerto Rico. During the early evening of 31 October 1641, the ship grounded on a reef and came to a shuddering halt. Efforts to get her free of the reef were futile and in desperation the men set to work to build rafts. As soon as they were completed, these rafts, crowded with survivors, set out on a southerly course, hoping to reach Puerto Rico. The casualties on that last leg of their journey were enormous. It is estimated that the *Concepción* had accommodated 500 passengers and

Treasure hunters, however, are a breed apart. They see encouragement where other men see nothing but disappointment. An unsuccessful voyage serves only to make the next voyage seem more promising and Phips could hardly wait to get started with his. Around New Providence there was much talk of a wreck on the reefs of the extreme south-east Bahamas, a wreck that had never been found and which contained many tons of silver. And therein he saw where his chance lay.

Phips undoubtedly talked with anyone he could find who had sailed in that area to the north of Hispaniola. And he came to realise that it was a lonely and treacherous patch of God's sea. The area was marked by extensive shallow banks studded with perilous coral reefs of terrifying sound and appearance. Ships sailing

A Spanish galleon similar to the Concepción.

crew, and of these 300 were lost during the storm, shipwreck and subsequent efforts to reach land. And, of course, all of the treasure was lost except some small amounts that survivors might have taken with them.

The loss of the silver was a severe blow to the Spanish treasury and many efforts were made to locate the wreck, but all were in vain. The remains of the *Concepción* and its precious cargo could not be found. Now, 42 years after that fateful night, William Phips had persuaded Charles II, King of England, to lend his support to a new search. The King's contribution to the enterprise was to supply a well-found ship. The *Rose of Algeree* which the King loaned Phips was armed with 18 guns and could accommodate a hundred men, and the rough and unlettered New Englander was mighty proud to be captain of a man-of-war.

He sailed first to Boston, tarried there for some weeks, and then to New Providence, arriving there on 9 February 1684. He found Charles Towne almost empty of inhabitants and in disarray, for it had been only 21 days prior to his arrival that the Spaniards had sacked the place.[1] Nevertheless, it is likely that by that time the privateers had once again set up shop in their favourite harbour and Phips was able to obtain the supplies he needed.

Phips must have looked on the disconsolate scene presented by Charles Towne with many misgivings. Had he not spent so much time in Boston he might have met with the small Spanish force that had invaded New Providence and he would have liked that. For no one could doubt his bravery and loyalty; with his bare fists he could quell an armed mutiny, as he was to demonstrate. And, after all, he and the King were business partners. To have saved one of the King's possessions from Spanish depradation would have brought him honour which he craved even more than silver.

But all that was past and there was a job ahead. He put his men to work on the wreck near New Providence which he had 'fished' before. This was important in breaking in his crew but the financial results were as ungratifying as they had been on the first try. After a few weeks, however, he set sail for the south-eastern Bahamas where his great hope lay.

To put it briefly, the voyage was a failure. Months of searching the terrifying reef-strewn area did not reveal the Spanish wreck. But Phips had learned much, including the certainty that he had been on the wrong bank; the wreck was surely on a bank further to the east! With that undying hope, characteristic of treasure hunters, he was anxious to get back to England and organise another voyage.

On arriving there he hoped to get royal backing for the next attempt as he had had for the last. However, Charles II had died and his brother and successor, James II, showed no interest in the venture.

The Duke of Albemarle.

Failing to secure the support of the man who sat on the throne, Phips next turned his attention to a man close to the throne, the Duke of Albemarle. This duke, Christopher Monk, was the son of George, the first Duke of Albemarle, who had been largely responsible for the Restoration and was incidentally, also a Lord Proprietor of The Bahamas.

Albemarle had been, in many respects, a kindred soul to Charles II. He gambled to excess and entertained lavishly. As a result he saw the great fortune which he had inherited dwindle to the point where he was compelled to sell off some of his best properties. And he, again like Charles II, was anxious to take a long shot in a gamble that might bring a windfall.

With Albemarle as the chief investor, Phips found it easy to get the rest of the necessary capital. Two vessels were purchased, one a ship of 200 tons which was renamed the *James and Mary* and the other, the *Henry*, a 40-ton sloop. On 12 September 1686 this small fleet set sail for the silver 'fishing' grounds.

A little under four months later, Rogers, captain of the *Henry*, was on the bank which Phips had concluded was the last resting place of the *Concepción*. In small boats they searched a portion of the reef for a whole day without success. The next day, 20 January 1687, the boats had been gone but two hours when they returned in a joyous mood. They had found the wreck! And they had with them thousands of pieces of eight to prove it!

In life it is interesting to consider what a very thin line sometimes separates success from failure. A man in one of the small boats scanning the sea bottom with his water glass had sighted a gorgeous growth of coral, probably a sea-fan, and had asked a diver to get it for him as a souvenir of the voyage. The diver came back to report that he had seen cannons on the bottom and other signs of a wreck. And that was it.

After Phips arrived a few days later, divers of the two vessels were kept busy at the fishing for the next three months whenever the weather permitted. In those days 'fishing for silver' was the accepted phrase to describe salvage of this kind. And, in fact, the procedure was, in some ways, similar to normal fishing. A canvas bucket, suspended on a hook, was lowered to the bottom by a piece of rope. After divers had filled the container, they would tug on the rope, rather like a fish biting, as a signal to those in the boat to haul it up. The bucket was emptied and thrown over again to await the next strike.

On this venture, neither on the outward nor homeward voyage did the ships stop at New Providence. Had they done so Phips would have seen devastation in Charles Towne far worse than that which had met his eyes in February of 1684. For the Spaniards had struck again in November of that year and Charles Towne was completely destroyed.[2]

The *James and Mary* and *Henry* were luckier with their precious cargo than the *Concepción* had been over 40 years before. They arrived home without misadventure.

The weight of the silver treasure was over 68,000 pounds troy. In addition there was a small amount of gold, jewellery and precious stones. James II must have felt extremely annoyed with himself for not investing in the venture, but even so he received over £20,000 which represented the King's tenth. On an investment of £800 the Duke of Albemarle's share was over £45,000. Captain Phips with £11,000 seems to have been underpaid, but there was more than money in store for him.

Captain Sir William Phips.

Medal commemorating the successful voyage of Sir William Phips. On one side a portrait of King James II and his daughter Mary of Modena and on the other a picture of the divers in the foreground and the Concepción *in the background.*

A medal was struck in commemoration of the voyage and discovery. Phips was knighted by the King on 25 June 1687 and later he was to be made Governor of Massachusetts. But throughout all his good fortune The Bahamas must have remained very much in his mind. And now that he was an English knight, he felt particularly irked by Spanish invasions in Bahamian waters, the last of which had resulted in the destruction of Charles Towne.

For some reason or other he had become attracted to 'the island which makes the harbour'. Perhaps he wanted it as a base for future treasure hunting expeditions. However that may be, he wanted it so badly that he was prepared to lay out £1,000 to secure the grant.

The Bahamian Grand Council was a powerful body in The Bahamas, fully authorised to 'lett, sett, convey and assure' lands. It comprised five Deputies of the Lords Proprietors and five members chosen from the Assembly.[3]

It was to this Council that Sir William Phips applied for a grant of the island. In return, he offered to spend the generous sum of £1,000 on defences of New Providence. In addition, Phips no doubt counted on the magic of his now famous name and his favour with the King and Albemarle.

Even from a pragmatic point of view, the Grand Council must have been seriously tempted by Phips's proposal. No matter who owned the island it would still 'make the harbour'; and the evidence was clear that defence against Spanish invasion was the most sorely needed improvement if New Providence was ever to make progress. But for all that, Phips was to be disappointed. The Grand Council refused his proposal, explaining that the island was to be kept as a commonage for the inhabitants of New Providence.[4]

3
Nicholas Trott

Sir William Phips, as we have seen, was the first man to apply for a grant of 'the island which makes the harbour'. Considering that Bahamian land was worth very little at the time, his offer was generous, but it was refused. Now we will consider a man who applied for and was granted the island on terms which were generous on the part of the Proprietors.

But to follow the mainstream of events we have to turn once more to New Providence. Charles Towne, the settlement which had developed there, was sacked in January 1684 and completely destroyed by the Spaniards in November of the same year. The inhabitants, seeing no hope of leading a decent and secure life in New Providence, left the island for other parts, chiefly Jamaica.

Governor Lilburne was faced with a despairing situation. Charles Towne was burnt to the ground and most of the people who might have rebuilt it had fled the island. He was a governor with nothing and nobody to govern. He could see no sense in remaining among the pine trees and at the first opportunity he took passage for London.

For the next two years New Providence remained practically uninhabited. On 1 December 1686 a new and unusual group of settlers arrived.[1] Their leader was Thomas Bridges, 'a conventional preacher'. They had come from Jamaica and among the group were some who had quitted New Providence two years before. Bridges was elected 'President' of the island by the people who came with him. The freebooters quickly moved in to join the group and nothing seemed to go right. The Governor of Barbados, writing to England, stated that there were in New Providence 'some small settlements... made by a rude sort of piratical and ungoverned people'.[2]

The Lords Proprietors eventually confirmed Bridges as Governor but soon after that they fired him, having concluded that he was not the man to set New Providence on an even keel. His successor was Cadwallader Jones.

Jones, appointed in November of 1689, proved to be an arrogant man who openly consorted with pirates and allowed them to do much as they pleased.[3] A description of his dishonest deeds, misgovernment and trickery would exhaust the vocabulary of tyranny. It staggers the mind to understand how he could have remained in office for three years. He was dismissed in January 1693, and Nicholas Trott appointed in his stead. One of the new Governor's first acts was to make Jones a member of his Council.

Nicholas Trott was born on 15 April 1658[4] and had grown up on his father's estate at Hog Bay, Bermuda. The reason for the name Hog is not difficult to guess, for the first people to settle there found the islands overrun with wild hogs. And perhaps at that particular bay they were exceptionally plentiful. It was a good place to secure the family's Sunday dinner.

The Trotts were of some assistance in the settling of Bermudians in New Providence and they naturally retained an interest in the fortunes and misfortunes of the new colony.

In 1691 Nicholas Trott was in London engaged in a legal battle with Isaac Richier, Governor of Bermuda.[5] The litigation had to do with one of Trott's ships, laden with tobacco, on which duty had not been paid. Consequently, the Governor had seized the vessel and cargo. By the time the ship was released, the tobacco had rotted and Trott had gone to England to seek redress.

Trott could get no satisfaction and was financially set back on his haunches. At that time the Lords Proprietors of The Bahamas were anxious to be rid of Governor Cadwallader Jones, and they offered the job to Trott. He accepted, hoping in some way to be able to recoup his fortune in that young and boisterous colony. He arrived at New Providence in August 1694 with important work ahead, including the building of a new town and a fort. Apparently the Proprietors had decided to try once again to make something of their troublesome and unprofitable Bahamian grant. A town of 160 houses and a church was designed to take the place of Charles Towne.[6] The fort, mounting 28 guns, 'was constructed on the site of the present Sheraton British Colonial Hotel. Both town and fort were named Nassau in honour of the Prince of Orange-Nassau who then sat on the English throne as William III.

The 'island which makes the harbour' stood bold before Trott's eyes every day as he superintended the building of the town. It is likely that he visited it frequently and gave much thought to its possibilities.

The name 'Hog' first appears during his term of office and we are justified in believing that he was responsible for the cognomen.[7] Perhaps he chose the name because of a sentimental attachment to the Hog Bay of his more youthful days. This hypothesis with respect to the name is reinforced, but not confirmed, by another Hog Island and another Trott. A cousin and namesake of this Governor, Nicholas Trott the younger, migrated to Carolina and soon became prominent in the affairs of that colony. In turn he held the posts of Attorney-General, Speaker and Chief Justice, wielding 'a power in one man never heard of before'.[8] In our research we came across the fact that there had been a small island near Charleston which, as early as 1694, bore the name of Hog. We wrote to George C Rogers, Professor of History, University of South Carolina, pointing out the coincidence of the two Hog Islands and the possible common origin of the name. He replied, 'I think you are probably correct in thinking there is a link in the names of Hog Island in The Bahamas and Hog Island in Carolina, with a Bermuda origin.' Incidentally, the Carolina Hog Island is now completely washed away while the Bahamian Hog Island stands firm.

Apart from building a town and a fort, Trott was absorbed with certain matters which cast a suspicious light on his honesty and fitness for the gubernatorial post.[9]

In the spring of 1695 the *Jufron Gertrud*, a Dutch ship, struck a reef near New Providence and remained grounded for 22 days. Trott seized her cargo, valued at $2,300, 'for safe keeping'.[10]

Apparently he kept it so safely that the owners could not get it back. The Dutch ambassador complained to the Proprietors who ordered Trott to make good the loss. Being unable to comply, he appealed to the House of Lords and lost the case. As a result he was later forced to spend a part of 1702 in the Fleet Prison in London.

A year after the *Jufron Gertrud* incident, another vessel came along to heap more troubles on the Governor's head.

On 1 April 1696 a fine ship, the *Fancy*, of 46 guns had anchored off Royal Island. The captain, who gave the name of Henry Bridgeman, sent a message to the Governor requesting permission to enter Nassau harbour. There were 200 men on board, he said, and they were out of provisions. Furthermore, the vessel was in need of repairs.[11]

Trott was faced with a suspicious and frightening situation. It was difficult to believe that a vessel so heavily armed and manned was a trader. But what could he do? If he refused permission, the captain might very well decide to enter anyway. And he had not the force to stop him. Fort Nassau was not yet finished and there were not more than 60 men in the whole of New Providence 'and many of them not fit for service'.

Bridgeman was given permission to enter the harbour. Some days later the Governor and the Council decided that his arrival at Nassau, whether he was a pirate or not, might have been providential. News was received that a French force of three ships and 320 men had seized the island of Exuma and had then made ready to descend on Nassau. But *en route* they met with a Bahamian vessel whose captain informed them that a great English ship with 200 men aboard had recently arrived at New Providence. The French commander thereupon turned about and sailed away.

Captain Avery and his crew taking one of the Great Mogul's ships.

Some months later, Trott learned that the ship, *Fancy*, was indeed a pirate vessel and that the captain was not Bridgeman but Henry Avery, the most notorious pirate of the day. Avery was no coastal pirate or small-time thief. Prior to coming to The Bahamas he had been on a cruise to the Indian Ocean where he had taken a ship belonging to the Great Mogul. There were many distinguished Muslims on board on the first leg of a pilgrimage to Mecca. But more exciting for the pirates was a veritable fortune in gold, silver, ivory and gems that was destined to adorn the shrine of the Prophet. Avery then designed to sail to a place where he might divide the booty and let each man disappear to whatever safe haven he could find. And in Nassau he did just that.

The extent to which Trott became involved with the pirates is somewhat ambiguous. It seems certain that he entertained them at Government House. One of the pirate crew, in a later testimony, said that the Governor 'gave them a treat at his house at which one of the men breaking a drinking glass was made to pay for it eight chequers (£3. 12. 0)'. Others swore that Trott received a sum of money for every pirate allowed ashore and that the *Fancy*, after the valuables were removed, was given to him by Avery as a present.

The Proprietors found Trott's conduct unsavoury. He was relieved of his job on 9 November 1696[12] and told to come home. But at that time he went no further than Bermuda.

None of the Lords Proprietors ever visited The Bahamas. The nearest that any one of them came to Nassau was when Albemarle went to Jamaica as Governor, shortly before his death.[13] Nevertheless, it was necessary for them to be informed of what was going on in their troublesome colony, and to achieve this they appointed agents who resided in Nassau.

During Trott's time the two most important men in Nassau were Messrs Amy and Thornton. Edward Randolph, Surveyor General of Customs in America reported that the Lords Proprietors were 'wholly unacquainted with their true interest and benefit and were entirely actuated by Amy and Thornton, their chief managers'.[14]

Amy was a London grocer who had come to the New World to seek his fortune.[15] Apparently he was doing very well by the end of the seventeenth century. He had acquired 12,000 acres in Carolina, was thought well enough of by the Proprietors of The Bahamas to be appointed as an agent, and was later to be a Proprietor of Carolina himself. He had a daughter by the name of Anne to whom Trott became romantically attached. Two years after being fired as Governor of The Bahamas, Nicholas Trott and Anne were married.[16]

In the same year as his marriage (1698), Trott was back in England. No doubt, his primary purpose in going there was to defend himself in the lawsuit concerning the Dutch ship, the *Jufron Gertrud*. But he lost no time in approaching the Lords Proprietors about a matter which obviously had been in his head for a long time. He applied for a grant of Hog Island.

He must have known of the reason why Phips had been turned down when he made a similar request. But Trott had a powerful advocate in the person of Amy, his father-in-law, and that proved to be the key to his success.

Trott had played his cards well. There is no doubt that had he applied to the Grand Council in Nassau, as Phips had done, his application would have been refused for the same reason. But, comfortably settled in England, he went straight to 'the head of the stream', the Lords Proprietors who were not so well acquainted with the feelings of the Nassau people, or did not care about them. On 30 September 1698, the Proprietors sold the island to Trott for £50, plus an annual rental of one shilling per 100 acres.[17]

Soon after Trott had secured possession of the island, the Deputies and the Council in Nassau, probably suspecting that something was afoot, passed an Act making Hog Island a free common. A letter from the Proprietors, dated 21 September 1699, disallowed this Act 'because we had granted the island to Colonel Nicholas Trott before'.[18]

When news of the transaction reached Nassau it provoked a storm of protest. An address by the inhabitants to King and Parliament, dated 1701, read in part:

last year [the Proprietors] sold an island, which by our Assembly was often confirmed as a common to the city of Nassau, and conveyance signed by those that had power from the Proprietors to grant all their other lands, besides it makes the Harbour.[19]

Another letter written the same year to the Lords Commissioners for Trade, stated:

These inhabitants are daily more unsettled and will give little credit to what their Lordships say or promise them they will do for their encouragement when at the same time they sell and dispose of their privileges for very inconsiderable sums, as Hog Island, lying to the northward of Providence, which makes the Harbour, 'tis, after several grants and confirmation thereof to the inhabitants, sold to Mr Trott for 50 pounds, to the utter ruin to the Inhabitants of the Town.[20]

The indefatigable Randolph, Surveyor General of Customs in America, also frowned on the transaction. He railed about proprietary governors:

who enrich themselves by all unjust practices. I mention Mr Trott as chief, all of which, and a great deal more, I found verifyed in him. Mr Trott has married Mr Amy's daughter. Their Lordships, by Mr Amy's persuasion, have sold Mr Trott Hog Island, which makes Providence harbour, for £50, to the ruin of the inhabitants of Providence Island.[21]

From a similar complaint by John Graves, Collector of Customs, we learn that Hog Island had also been named Anne Island at some point but it is not certain whether it was named for Anne as daughter of James II (1685–1688) or when she became Queen in 1702. Trott's wife was also named Anne.[22]

The Governor of Boston was even more caustic in assessing Trott's character. 'If common fame lies not extremely,' he wrote '[Trott] is the greatest pirate-broker that was ever in America.'[23]

Indications are that Trott spent the rest of his life in London, much of it absorbed in litigious matter. There was the case of the Dutch ship which landed him in prison, and 'the old tussle with Richier which dragged on for another quarter of a century'.[24]

Woman pirate Anne Bonney.

4
Privateers, Pirates and Woodes Rogers

Nicholas Webb succeeded Trott to the governorship to preside over a dissatisfied and depressed colony.[1]

Hog Island had been lost as a common, the Treaty of Ryswick, 1697, had put an end to profitable privateering and the prices that could be obtained for salt and hardwood had fallen drastically. Webb, beset by troubles on every side, including many of his own making, decided the best thing he could do was to pack up and leave. And he did that without the formality of resigning.[2]

On arriving in Pennsylvania he met with misadventure. At Newcastle, he went ashore leaving his possessions on board ship. The crew 'with the assistance of several pirates' took the ship to sea, leaving Webb in town with nothing but the clothes on his back. Among his losses were £7,000 in cash and '£1,000 in rich goods'.[3] This was poetic justice of a sort, for one is left to wonder how this Governor could have amassed £8,000 in wealth when he had been in The Bahamas for only two years on an annual salary of £200.

When Webb 'eloped his office' he made arrangements for a 'mulatto', Read Elding, to carry on the duties of Governor. While still in office, Webb had sent Elding out to capture some pirates. Elding did not find the pirates but he brought back a ship which he had found crewless and drifting. And in collusion with Webb, he claimed her as flotsam. The deal was spoiled when the crew showed up a year later and the ship had to be returned to them.[4] The loss of the ship must have been a great disappointment to Elding and perhaps it was in compensation for this that Webb gave him the job of Deputy Governor.

This post was never confirmed by the Proprietors and Elding had only a short time to enjoy his position as head of the colony. During that brief period he was allowed to have the death sentence passed on four pirates and he presented a petition to the Lords Proprietors to allow Hog Island to be 'turned into common land'. The pirates were successfully hanged but the Hog Island request was denied, the Proprietors pointing out that they had already sold it to Trott.[5]

When Captain Elias Haskett was made Governor in April 1700, conditions in the colony seemed to be in an irreversible decline. The poor man was not allowed the privilege of 'eloping' his office as Webb had done. Oldmixon says that wrecking was scarce and pirates began to spend their money elsewhere. But 'whatever was the occasion, the inhabitants were in a little time so out of humour with Mr Haskett, that they seized him, put him in irons and sent him away'.[6]

By the beginning of the eighteenth century, it was clear enough that the clock of proprietary government was running down at an ever-increasing rate, but there were still a few feeble ticks left in the troublesome machine. Fort Nassau, which Trott had completed three or four years before, had rotted to the ground and no effort was made to rebuild it.[7] Consequently, Nassau was defenceless and constantly threatened by the Spaniards.

That the threats were not idle talk was demonstrated in October of 1703. In combination, French and Spanish forces sailed from Havana and descended on New Providence. The enemy proceeded to thoroughly sack and plunder Nassau; they spiked the guns, killed many of the men and, after a two-week stay, sailed away taking 80 persons including Acting Governor Lightwood with them.[8] The people who had hidden in the bush during the fortnight of terror quitted the island at the first opportunity.

A few months after the enemy had done its work, Edward Birch arrived as the new Governor, not having heard of the catastrophe:

> *but finding it a Desert, he did not give himself the Trouble to open his Commission. He tarried there two or three months and was all that while forced to sleep in the Woods. After which he came back, and left the Place uninhabited, as it remains at present: But it is expected, that as soon as the Government of the Island is settled, and Measures taken to defend it, the Wrecks and other Advantages will tempt People to venture upon a third Settlement.*[9]

Hoping to prevent that eventuality, the Spaniards returned the following year and again in 1706.

After this series of incursions there was precious little, if anything, left of the Nassau which Trott had built. On each occasion, the people who escaped capture or death hid in the woods until the immediate danger had passed. Thereafter, they either scattered to other places or set to work to build crude 'stick and thatch' huts for themselves. Thus, Nassau, to the despair of the Spaniards, proved to be like the many-headed Hydra of Greek mythology: when one head was cut off, two more quickly grew to take its place. Unfortunately, the propensity of the settlement to rise again from the ashes of its predecessor was not matched by a determination on the part of the Proprietors to make it secure.

Twenty years before, Sir William Phips had seen that a proper defence against enemy aggression was the most urgent need of Nassauvians. The £1,000 he was prepared to expend in that direction, in exchange for Hog Island, would have gone far towards making New Providence safe from Spanish raids. The Proprietors had rejected this proposal and had sold the island to Trott for £50 in 1698, as we have seen.

Fort Nassau, which Trott had built, must have been something of a joke. It was finished in 1697 and when Haskett arrived four years later he found it had rotted to the ground. We suspect it had been built of palmetto logs and white lime. Except for this miserable effort the Proprietors had done nothing to remove the fear of insecurity which hung like the sword of Damocles over the heads of the inhabitants, The destruction of Nassau was a painful blow to them as, with high expectations, they had invested much money in having that town built; a town which impressed Oldmixon as being 'as big as the cities of St James and St Mary's, in Maryland and Virginia'.[10]

Birch left New Providence in June of 1704 and his departure marked the end of proprietary government for all practical purposes. A few more feeble efforts were made to appoint governors but none ever reached The Bahamas.

Edward Teach, alias Blackbeard, one of the most notorious pirates who infested Nassau harbour.

During the 14 years from 1704 to 1718 an almost impenetrable darkness is drawn across Bahamian history. Nevertheless, flashes of light illuminate the scene from time to time, and from these brief flashes a pattern can be seen.

As far as the Nassau-based privateers were concerned, the collapse of government happily coincided with the War of the Spanish Succession. It was easy enough for them to get their 'letters of marque' from nearby governments, which allowed private ships to wage war against the enemy, and their booty could be disposed of legally and to the best advantage in Nassau without government interference. As might be expected, under these conditions, privateers proliferated. And those who took a farsighted view of the situation recognised the fact that the privateering school afforded the best training field for pirates. To make the transition, there were additional risks, but nothing new had to be learned. Thus, when a particularly tempting prize appeared, or when the pickings were lean, the privateers crossed the line which separated them from piracy with the greatest of ease.

In 1714 peace was declared – a mortal blow to the livelihoods of genuine privateers. They could no longer plunder French and Spanish ships without the fear of the hangman's noose. And so scores of these seamen who had lived a hazardous, but legitimate life now switched to piracy to earn a living. Furthermore, many of the seasoned pirates of the western world, hounded out of their habitual ports and wanting 'some place of retreat, where they might lodge their wealth, clean and repair their ships and make themselves some kind of abode,' flocked to Nassau.[11]

Since the beginning of proprietary government, New Providence and, to a lesser extent, the rest of The Bahamas, had experienced nothing but an increasingly dark record of disaster. By 1717 the colony had reached the bottom and utter degradation. The two or three hundred peaceful inhabitants lived in fearful anxiety; fearful of disease which was rampant, fearful of the Spaniards who made periodic assaults on their property and lives, and fearful of the domineering and cruel pirates.

The pirates at that time numbered more than a thousand ashore and afloat, and the atrocities they committed would numb the mind just to read of them. There is, for instance, one incident concerning Trott's nephew's wife which can be related, especially since we are spared the gory details. From a letter written in 1709 describing some of the atrocities of the pirates, we read 'and they killed Mr Perrion Trott's wife in a most barbarous manner with their cruelties, to make her confess where Colonel Elding and his riches were'.[12]

It is obvious that conditions existing in Nassau not only nullified law and order, but every progressive idea suggested during those unhappy days. If Nicholas Trott had conceived of a plan for the use of Hog Island, it had to remain dormant. The killing of his nephew's wife, no doubt, affected him deeply and it must have destroyed any ambitions he might have had in that direction. But during this period the ex-Governor was far removed from Hog Island and its scene of tribulations. He was in London, embroiled in troublesome litigation.

The situation in The Bahamas had reached the point where it could no longer be ignored by the British authorities. The chief fault was seen to lie in the inept and corrupt governors that the Proprietors invariably appointed. They had neither the ability nor the character to deal fairly with the residents, to rid New Providence of pirates and other unsavoury elements, to maintain internal and external security, or to establish a viable plantation.

Most of the decent inhabitants had quitted the capital, leaving behind an assorted crew of vagabonds to do as they pleased. As a result, the House of Lords suggested to the King that a reversal of the chaotic downward trend might be achieved by appointing a royal governor, a man who would be answerable only to the British authorities in matters relating to security and government.

Fortunately, at that time, a sea captain and ex-privateer, Woodes Rogers, was looking for the kind of employment that might offer a challenge to his brave and determined spirit. He applied for and was granted the governor's job and he and some co-partners leased

Captain Woodes Rogers landing on the coast of California during his three-year journey round the world.

and who knew very well that the Governor had come to put them out of business.

To the assembled crowd, Rogers then read his own commission and the King's pardon to penitent pirates. The latter document said, in effect, that those pirates who, on oath, forswore their way of life within a limited time would be pardoned for past offences. Of those in port at the time, more than 300 took the oath.[16]

The Governor then let it be known that he would deal severely with any of the pardoned rogues who recanted. And he was as good as his word. On the morning of 12 December 1718, nine men who had received the pardon and who then had returned to their criminal way of life, were hanged on the seafront of Fort Nassau.[17] This determined action effectively ended the pirate menace.

No sooner had he dealt with the pirates, than word came to his ears that the Spanish were planning another of their habitual descents on New Providence. Faced with a shortage of every kind of material, he laboured night and day to place the capital island in a reasonable posture of defence. Fort Nassau was rebuilt, a battery was positioned to guard the eastern entrance to the harbour, a garrison was established and lookouts, on regular watch, were positioned at vulnerable points. In all, Rogers had about 500 men, including ex-pirates, at his disposal, a large number of whom were drunk or otherwise incapable, at any given time.[18]

The Spanish invasion fleet appeared on the northern horizon during the early morning of 24 February 1720. It comprised one frigate, three smaller warships and eight transport sloops carrying 1,500 soldiers.[19] Two armed ships in the harbour and the bristling cannon of Fort Nassau persuaded the Commander that it would be hazardous to attempt a direct attack, and the fleet came to anchor outside the bar. Thereafter, some of the

the Bahamian land from the Lords Proprietors for 21 years.[13]

Some years before coming to The Bahamas, Rogers had organised and led a three-year privateering expedition around the world. He returned to England laden with the wealth of a Spanish galleon and a castaway he had rescued from a Pacific island. The marooned man, Alexander Selkirk, later became the main character in Daniel Defoe's tale of *Robinson Crusoe*.[14] During his cruise, Rogers had proved to be a dauntless and resourceful commander. His reputation for cool courage was well known in The Bahamas, and there was no doubt that he would provide a refreshing change from his predecessors.

He landed at New Providence on 27 July 1718, a date of great importance in Bahamian history. His point of debarkation was the sea rocks in front of Fort Nassau where the Sheraton British Colonial Hotel now stands. The pirates, whether from humour or respect, had formed a double file, a guard of honour, and as Rogers walked between the two lines, the pirates saluted him with a fusillade of musketry fire.[15] What Rogers thought of this strange reception is not recorded. But it must have taken a great deal of nerve to walk among those armed cut-throats to whom murder was second nature

Woman pirate Mary Reade.

Woodes Rogers, his son and daughter at New Providence, 1729. On the cartouche on the wall is written the family motto: Dum spiro spero *(While I breathe, I hope).*

smaller vessels sailed along the north coast of Hog Island and came to a stop near the Narrows. During the dark hours of the 25th, some small boats, crowded with troops, attempted a landing to the east of Nassau. 'But two valiant negro sentries blazed hotly and happily away at the oncoming boats.'[20] The Spaniards, having no appetite for the bullets that were ripping among them, withdrew in alarm. Apparently a similar attempt was made at putting troops ashore to the west of Nassau, but there, Rogers had placed ex-pirates as sentries and the enemy received the same hot reception that had greeted them in the east. The Commander finally sailed away convinced that Nassau was no longer the easy picking that it used to be.

But in the process of bringing New Providence to this degree of security, Rogers had exhausted his money and his health. He needed to get away from the trials and tribulations of Nassau. Before leaving, however, he wrote to Samuel Buck, agent for the co-partners, and asked him to press for more guns in Nassau and a battery for Hog Island.

In a memorial addressed to the Lords Commissioners of Trade and Plantations, Buck wrote of the suppression of piracy and the turning back of the last attempted Spanish invasion. He stressed the fact that the enemy 'yet continues to threaten to take this island [New Providence] by ye latest accounts we have from them. We find it necessary for ye security of ye harbour to have a Fort built on Hog Island of about 12 large cannon'.[21]

It is unlikely that any attempt was made to effect these recommendations.

5

From Phenney to Dunmore

Georoge Phenney, who succeeded to the governorship, fell far short of the calibre of Rogers. However he did have the advantage of being freed from many of the anxieties that troubled his predecessor's mind. He could, therefore, turn his thoughts to other matters that appealed to his sense of duty.

On the lighter side, the naturalist, Mark Catesby, visited Government House during this time and was understandably surprised at some of the activities of its occupants. While the Governor and Commander-in-Chief were examining his bare feet for chiggers in the parlour, Mrs Phenney was selling rum and biscuits at the back door.[1]

In general though, the new Governor advanced the good work which Rogers had set in motion. 'Many families came and settled, who by their industry and improvement upon their plantations furnished the markets with all sorts of provisions'.[2]

Soon after Phenney's arrival, Lord Carteret, one of the Proprietors, presented an unusual request to Governor Nicholson of South Carolina. A Mr Carrington, he explained, was anxious to 'have the liberty to transport 15 or 20 brace of deer for breed, from South Carolina to Hog Island,' and 'I recommend it to you to satisfy him in this request'.[3] What Governor Nicholson thought of this request we do not know, but there is no record of Carolina deer being introduced to the exotic environment of Hog Island.

Perhaps Phenney never heard of the plan to introduce deer, but he did know of some common species of livestock which were then breeding very well on the island. A proclamation of his Council issued in 1723 draws attention to the fact that 'several ill-disposed and disorderly people have from time to time shot, killed and destroyed great numbers of sheep, goats, hoggs and other livestock...on Hog Island and other small islands and keys belonging to this Government

where they have been put by several of our well meaning and industrious subjects with a view of increase of our public good'.[4] The proclamation goes on to offer a £10 reward for information leading to the conviction of anyone engaged in such illegal activities.

The wheels of industry were beginning to turn again and the population of New Providence had increased to 750. Phenney could see that Hog Island, if properly utilised, could be of benefit to the growing colony. And on 1 October 1722 he placed the matter before his Council, which arrived at the following decision:

> *It being generally accepted and taken that Hog Island is a key that lies opposite to the town of Nassau and forms the harbour of Providence, is most commodious for the grazing and raising of livestock much wanted here, and Colonel Trott the supposed owner not having made or ordered any settlement thereon. The Governor and Council thought it but reasonable to have the said Hog Island made use of for the Public good of the Government.*
>
> *Therefore Agreed, Resolved and ordered that till it appears from England who has the property of Hog Island, the same be occupied accordingly. And the usual quit rent to be reserved for the claims of the right owner to be paid by such person who shall possess the same or any part of it.*
>
> *Ordered also that for the future no person whatsoever to land and go upon Hog Island with either gun or dog without leave first granted.*[5]

This Council resolution clearly suggests that Trott had done nothing with Hog Island since he purchased it 23 years before, as we surmised. Whether, during those tumultuous years, he had paid the annual rent of six or seven shillings a year we are unable to say. Nevertheless, it must have come to his ears in England that the bad days in The Bahamas were over and that Governor Phenney was showing a lively interest in the island which he looked upon as his own.

Consequently, he joined forces with Richier, the former Governor of Bermuda, and the two instructed their Nassau attorneys to press their claims to a considerable amount of Bahamian real estate, including Hog Island. How these two became allies in this pursuit we cannot say, for at that particular time, as far as we know, they were engaged in a fierce legal battle concerning the shipload of tobacco which Richier had caused Trott to lose.

We have the feeling that Phenney became a little tired of this importuning. In a letter to Lord Carteret he spoke of Trott's and Richier's persistence and then explained his own view of the matter:

I have generally answered that when any such claimants produce authentic copies of the original assignments from the Lords Proprietors they shall be admitted, but I presume they will be obliged to settle those great tracts of lands they claim to provide for their defence according to the tenor of the usual patents.[6]

Obviously the next move which Trott had to make was to present proof of his grants. But he was getting on in years then, very close to the three score and ten mark and probably too old to contemplate an Atlantic voyage, so he sent his son Perrient to Nassau with his power of attorney to act on his behalf.

Apparently the name Perrient was well liked by the Trotts. It was the given name of Nicholas's father, of his nephew whose wife had been killed by pirates and of his son mentioned above.

Perrient Trott presented a lengthy list of properties to the Governor and Council which met on 9 January 1727. They included:

1 Hog Island.
2 300 acres joining or butting the western wall of Nassau.
3 Two plantations of 250 acres, each five miles to the west of Nassau.
4 Four building lots in town.
5 A 60-foot lot on the waterfront.
6 One half of the island of Exuma.

In addition, Perrient also produced a copy of an exclusive grant of a licence from the Lords Proprietors for 31 years, to cut all the wood or timber on all the Bahama Islands.[7] This list shows quite clearly that Trott used his position as Governor and his alliance with Amy to enhance his own fortunes.

With the exception of Hog Island, all the other claims were supported by witnesses or unattested grants or assignments. But the claim to Hog Island was supported by a copy of the grant, 'proved before the Lord Mayor of London and two Notaries Public', and 'bearing date the 30th September, 1698'.

Subsequent mention of the Governor and Council meetings is silent on the decision regarding Trott's claim, but it should be pointed out that some of these minutes are missing.

After Phenney, Woodes Rogers returned for a second time as Governor, and after him there were six other governors before Lord Dunmore arrived on the scene in 1787.

John Tinker was Governor for 20 years (1738–1758), the longest term of any man before or since. Britain was at war during the greater part of his administration[8] and Nassau rode the crest of a privateering boom. In 1748, he observed that New Providence had 'increased most surprisingly in strength and wealth and the town of Nassau grown populous'. He added that the war had introduced 'two formidable enemies – luxury and sloth – the excessive dearness of every necessary of life would make a stranger at first sight imagine we had golden mines no farther off than the Blue Hills'.[9]

The real gold mines, of course, were the privateering vessels. And in Tinker's time, as in times before, preying on enemy commerce engendered the threat of revenge. Thus, immediately after his arrival, Tinker had Fort Montagu constructed and Fort Nassau rebuilt. And casting his eyes across the harbour he saw Hog Island as the weak spot in the defences, as Rogers had recognised it to be 20 years before. In a letter to the Lords Commissioners of Trade and Plantations, dated June 1743, he asked for the funds to erect 'a small battery upon the point of Hog Island'.[10]

In 1765 the matter of a battery on Hog Island was again taken up – this time by Tinker's successor, William Shirley. The Commander of a naval sloop was asked by Shirley to prepare an estimate of cost for the defence project. 'Allowing 12 men to work on it,' wrote the Commander, 'it may be executed in three months which together with materials of timber, stone, mortar, tools, ironwork, nails, mahogany plank, boats and flatts to carry the necessaries that are wanted, will cost about £300.'[11]

After the wars and privateering, New Providence fell into a slump of the greatest severity. The Treasury was bankrupt. For lack of funds the Assembly refused to authorise a militia, or even a night watch. There were only 13 men to garrison Forts Nassau and Montagu and the Public Treasury could scarcely afford the £20 a month to keep them employed. The courts of law were forced to close down and the salaries of officials could not be paid.[12]

Commodore Esek Hopkins. Commander-in-Chief of the American fleet which captured New Providence, 1776.

Then came the American Revolutionary War with all its disrupting influences. On the military side, New Providence was invaded in 1776 by the newly assembled American navy under the command of Commodore Esek Hopkins.[13] Hopkins discovered to his chagrin, however, that the gunpowder so badly needed by the rebels, and the object of his mission, had been shipped out of Nassau before he had the opportunity to seize it. He stayed on in Nassau for two weeks, collected what war materials he could find and set sail for home.

Governor William Shirley (1758–1768).

LEFT: Photograph of oil painting of MAJOR SAMUEL NICHOLAS, Senior Marine Officer of the American Revo... The inscription on the reverse side reads: "Probably painted from a miniature presented to the Marine Co... 1921 by DR. J. NICHOLAS, his great-grandson, of Germantown, Pennsylvania, U.S.A. Artist: A. M. KOSINSKY. Defence Department photograph (Marine Corps) 523394 GS."

ABOVE: Photograph of official map of the raid of Continental Marines under the command of CAPTAIN SAMUEL NIC... upon Fort Montagu and Nassau, New Providence, March 1776. ADMIRAL HOPKINS of the newly-born Am... Navy led the expedition, consisting of eight ships, which dropped anchor at Salt Cay Anchorage. The town surren... when it was known that the sole purpose of the invasion was to remove the powder and ammunition from the forts...

Major Samuel Nicholson and map of first American raid in 1776.

New Providence was raided two years later by Captain Rathbun, utilising a single sloop. This raid was executed during the dark hours with such exquisite strategy and stealth that Nassauvians did not realise that anything was amiss until the following morning when they awoke to see the American Stars and Stripes flying over Fort Nassau and the massive guns of that bastion pointing at the town. The residents were obviously in a state of consternation, 'many of them were moving their goods out of their houses, either inland or over to Hog Island, apparently fearing seizure by the Americans'.[14] We can assume from this that Hog Island was habitually used as a hiding place for valuables during foreign incursions or invasions.

Finally, in 1782 the island was taken by the Spanish from Havana, with American help. A Spanish governor and a Spanish garrison occupied the capital for ten months at the end of which time it was brilliantly recaptured by Colonel Andrew Deveaux of the South Carolina Militia.[15]

On the economic side, during the Revolutionary War, there was a resurgence of privateering which compensated somewhat for the disruption of peaceful commerce.

Ann Maria Verplank (Mrs Andrew Deveaux II).

Britain lost the war and many of those colonists who had fought for a United Empire were either banished from their home states or no longer wanted to live there. Some thousands came to The Bahamas so that they might still live under the Union Jack. The British Government, feeling a responsibility to get these people resettled, gave them money to partially recompense their losses and free land on which to start a new life.

In 1717 when the Proprietors had surrendered the civil and military government to the Crown, they retained possession of the land. In fact, it was not until 1787 that the real estate was bought by the Crown for £12,000.[16] And only then could the Government grant it to the Loyalists. In the same year that the British Government repossessed the Bahama Islands, Lord Dunmore arrived to take up the post of Governor. And

Colonel Andrew Deveaux who recaptured Nassau from the Spaniards in 1783.

Lord Dunmore, Governor of The Bahamas (1786–1797). He divided Hog Island.

it fell to his lot to preside over the parcelling out of the land to genuine and deserving Loyalists.

Apparently, Dunmore's general non-conciliatory attitude had done much to harden the attitude of the American rebels during the Revolutionary War.[17] George Washington is reported to have recommended that he should be deprived of either his liberty or his life. The defeat of the British was a blow to Dunmore's patriotism and pride, especially since he was thought to have made a significant contribution to that defeat. Appointed Governor of The Bahamas in 1786, he arrived in Nassau the following year to exhibit the same truculence which had characterised his mainland administrations when he had been Governor of Virginia. Always autocratic and cantankerous, he crossed swords with many Bahamians, high and low.

When the British Government repurchased The Bahamas, the deal included the entire archipelago, except some bits and pieces that the Proprietors or their agents and lessees had previously granted to individuals. And Hog Island was not included among the exceptions. Apparently Trott's claim to the island as late as Phenney's time had not been thought valid.

Lord Dunmore, never one to forget himself when granting choice Crown land, selected two allotments on Hog Island totalling 240 acres. Two other grants to private persons were made, one to John Russell (300 acres) and one to Sarah Carmichael (35 acres); $18\frac{1}{4}$ acres were set aside for use by the War Department and $31\frac{3}{4}$ acres at the western end reserved as Crown land.[18]

Thus was Hog Island – 5.49 miles in length, 0.66 of a mile at its widest point, totalling 826 acres – broken up and, like Humpty Dumpty, unlikely ever to be put entirely together again. But time will tell.

Hermitage, County Seat of Lord Dunmore.

6

The War Department Land

An interesting map of Hog Island was prepared by Captain Andrew Skinner in 1788 at the instance of The Bahamas Assembly.[1] It must have been prepared just before Dunmore allocated the Loyalist grants, for there is no demarkation of boundaries. However, a few buildings and names are shown. 'I Kemp' and 'Chisolm' are the labels attached to two small structures which are obviously farm huts. Adjacent to the name 'Russell' are two buildings which were probably the beginnings of his shipyard business of which we will say more, later on. Another building, larger than the others, near the western end is labelled the 'Banqueting House'. And there is no reason to believe that it was used for any purpose other than that suggested by the name – a place where Nassauvians might repair for a day's picnic, and enjoy a repast in a cool cabana.

However, when Dunmore divided the island there was a flurry of activity in building defence works on the War Department land as one would expect, for he was determined that his new charge, The Bahamas, and especially New Providence, would not be lost as the mainland colonies had been. Furthermore, he probably had it in mind that New Providence had fallen to enemy invasions three times in recent years. And he did not want it to happen again. The necessity of fortifying Hog Island was readily seen by him as it had been by former governors, but being a nobleman, his appeals for money to the Home Government were more persuasive than those of his untitled predecessors.

In New Providence he built some durable forts, outstanding among which were Forts Charlotte and Fincastle which still stand as monuments to their robust construction.

In February of 1794 he wrote to the Secretary of State saying, among other things, that a battery of four 24-pounders 'had been erected on Hog Island in front of the town, as well to prevent the enemy from landing on that island, as to defend the entrance to the Eastward by Hanover Sound'.[2] Never one to be shy about perpetuating his name, Dunmore christened the battery Fort Murray. Additional structures which were built during Dunmore's governorship or soon after included a block house, a barracks which comprised three wooden buildings and a small hospital.

When Dunmore left the colony in 1796, John Forbes, a Loyalist, was appointed Acting Governor. However, he did not have many months to enjoy his high position. He contracted yellow fever and died the same year.[3] Thereupon, the President of the Council, Robert Hunt, assumed the reins of government.[4]

A military adviser by the name of Captain North recommended to Hunt that 'some person might be proper to take care of the Blockhouse and Battery at Hog Island… in order to keep any undisposed person from doing them damage by fire or spiking the guns, or other ways'.[5] But there being no military emergencies during those days, and money being perennially short, it seems that the defensive complex remained uncared for and unattended, and was left to rot.

Later in 1797 Captain Rutherford of the Royal Engineers wrote to the Secretary of State giving some new insights on the defensive importance of Hog Island as seen by him. 'The position of the island to any enemy', he stated, 'would facilitate all his operations – he might besides destroy the town and shipping from thence by erecting a battery on it'.[6]

Rutherford goes on to say that he had proposed three batteries and a blockhouse for the island and that two of

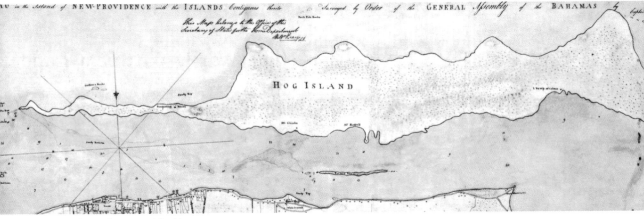

Skinner's map showing Hog Island in 1788.

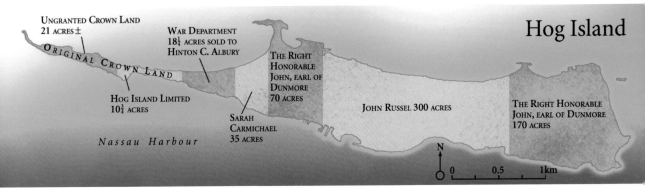

Hog Island as granted by Lord Dunmore.

the batteries and the blockhouse had been completed. Thus it would seem that Dunmore had built or started a second battery before his departure. The third battery had not been begun as Hunt, in his capacity as Acting Governor, did not deem himself authorised to proceed with the works without instructions from the Home Government.

The blockhouse, as Rutherford conceived it, would have served the purpose of a *tete de front* to preserve communication as far as possible with the island. Then he speaks of the most bizarre vessel that had ever been designed as a Nassau harbour ferry: 'a falling bridge to be made, with a marquet-proof breast-work, which was to have carried 100 men and two field pieces' to Hog Island.

This strange craft, which he called a gunboat, would also be capable of escorting and protecting a good number of sloops to any point, and would have been

very useful in securing a retreat from Hog Island. It is a great pity that no one ever made a sketch of this unusual craft which Rutherford said was almost completed. It must have looked like a cross between an ancient galley, an iron-clad gunboat of the Civil War era and a modern landing craft.

In 1783 no one could have foreseen that when the Spaniards surrendered to Deveaux it marked the last time that a foreign flag would fly over the capital as a symbol of dominion. Perhaps the defensive measures established by Lord Dunmore acted as a deterrent to aggression. Nevertheless, it does seem that as the nineteenth century wore on there was an increasing lack of interest in fortifications, and the existing works fell into decay.

However, as late as 1844 Governor Matthew attempted to restore the military effectiveness of Hog Island. He wrote to the English authorities explaining that 'at present bomb vessels might lay under the ridge of Hog Island, perfectly sheltered from our two incomplete forts [Nassau and Montagu], and hold the town which would be within easy range, entirely at their mercy'.[7]

He recommended the 'erection of a Water Battery and furnace [for heating the shot] together with a stone martello tower or fortified guard house, mounting two guns on Hog Island, at the same spot where the ruins of a former battery and fortification still exist.' Also mentioned were repairs needed to the fort at the eastern end of the island, commanding Cochraine's Anchorage.

The small hospital built on the War Department land, was designed to take care of casualties at the nearby blockhouse and Fort Murray in the event of an attack. But since there were no attacks and consequently no military casualties during its existence, other uses were found for the facility, as indicated by the following report:

> *On Thursday HMS Brig* Scout... *arrived from the coast of Cuba. Yesterday it was stated that her crew were in a most sickly state, and three of the officers having been landed and carried to the military hospital on the parade in this town, occasioned considerable sensation among the inhabitants. These sick persons having been removed to Hog Island in the course of the forenoon, the uneasiness which had been caused nearly subsided in the afternoon. We are informed that the Scout has within a short period lost upward of 20 men and 4 or 5 officers by the fever which has prevailed on board.*[8]

The residents of Nassau had every reason to be grateful for that small hospital on Hog Island for they knew the terror of infectious diseases. Twenty-six years before the incident described above, an epidemic of yellow fever had ravaged Nassau and carried off hundreds of people, including Acting Governor Forbes whom we met earlier.[9] The isolation provided by the Hog Island hospital undoubtedly protected the people of New Providence time and again when threatened with outbreaks of yellow fever, cholera, smallpox and typhoid. It bridged the gap between the times when nothing was done to prevent an epidemic and when proper isolation facilities were established at Athol Island.

An interesting epilogue to the story of the hospital is told by Mr Berdelle Key, who for many years worked with the West India Oil Company, then located at Hog Island on the former War Department land. Workers digging a hole in a sandy mound in which to bury some refuse, came across a number of skeletons. We may assume that some of these remains belonged to those who had died in isolation at the Hog Island hospital. Also, the area was sometimes used as a burial ground for epidemic victims who died in Nassau. In 1852 a news item stated that graves were dug on Hog Island for interment of victims of cholera, and some of the dead were buried there. 'After some protest from the Board of Health, the practice was discontinued'.[10]

It is unlikely that the barracks, comprising three wooden buildings, was ever filled with soldiers except, perhaps, when military exercises were held on the island. It seems, however, to have been used to accommodate some captive negroes in 1831. In the early part of that year a slaver was on the reef of Abaco. The wreckers who went to the ship were offered a substantial sum of money to take the slaves to an American port. They declined, perhaps partly from humane considerations and partly because they knew that in so doing they would run foul of British law. Consequently, the wretched captives were brought to Nassau. Owing to the circumstances of the situation the slave owners, hoping to regain their human cargo, petitioned the court. The captives were kept at Hog Island until the court's decision, which was to set them free.[11] It is most probable that they were housed in the barracks because there was no other facility on Hog Island which could accommodate them. Many captive slaves were being brought into Nassau harbour during those days and perhaps the Hog Island barracks was used for a similar purpose on other occasions.

A use of a different nature is described by an American physician who spent two years in Nassau. On a Saturday morning (24 January 1834), the Governor invited him and eight others 'on a maroon to the deserted barracks on Hog Island opposite the town'. A maroon was a kind of picnic in those days. The word was made popular by the pirates who sometimes put an unwanted man ashore on a desolate island, with little or no provisions, and left him there to survive or die as the fates would have it. In Nassau, in the physician's day, it meant to spend a day or half a day on some nearby uninhabited island with plenty of food and drink.

The physician's party left Nassau on the Governor's sailboat at 1.00 p.m. and debarked at the barracks two hours later. They:

> *walked over to the beach, admired the break and roar of the surf and the beautiful hard packed beach of finest snow-white sand and then walked back through the bay cedar bushes and wild grape and other shrubs which grow most luxuriantly on this barren soil, to one of the small buildings which compose the barracks. Here we found a fine collation spread and a cool pleasant shade. We sat down and after eating of salmon, corn beef, pickled oysters and drinking of good madeira, cider, etc., returned home.*[12]

What an enchanting way to be marooned!

There is nothing left on the War Department land to remind us of Dunmore or those who came after him. Perhaps excavations at the sandy mound would reveal the stone foundations of the blockhouse and the Fort Murray Battery. As late as 1932, one cannon of the battery could still be seen. Now there are none left, all having been moved to other fortifications or removed by wealthy residents for use as lawn ornaments.

It is not known whether the wooden buildings of the hospital and barracks yielded to termites and decay, whether they were pulled down when they became dilapidated or whether they survived to be swept away by the 1866 hurricane. Whatever happened to them, the War Department land, having outlived the usefulness that Dunmore had foreseen for it, was sold at public auction on the 13 February 1891 to Hilton C Albury.[13] Thereafter the story of this area is one of private enterprise.

7

The Crown Land

*T*he western tip of Hog Island is known as Hog Island Point. And if rocks could talk, that point would have some hair-raising tales to tell. But during the 'blood and thunder' days of our early history not much was written down and that which was, is lost.

A fragment of interest comes to us through the diary of an old Bahamian whose reminiscences begin in 1801. 'In former days', he writes, 'to which my recollection is faintly called, criminal blacks, after being hanged, were decapitated and placed on gibbet posts on Hog Island Point, about the site of the present lighthouse – and I think I have seen [the bleached bones] on the rocks, on which the decomposed matter had fallen, stand even for years after the head had been decomposed or tumbled to pieces'.[1]

However, for a long time before these ghastly scenes of which 'Old Bahamian' wrote, it was clearly seen that the Point could be used for an infinitely more salutary purpose than as a foundation for gibbets. In fact, the value of a lighthouse on the Point had probably been recognised since ships first began to enter Nassau harbour. Perhaps Lord Dunmore had a lighthouse in mind when he reserved the western end of Hog Island for the Crown, for we are informed that the idea had been 'long deliberated'.[2]

When Fort Fincastle, built on the highest elevation above Nassau, was completed in 1794, a lantern was affixed to its northern angle.[3] This was some improvement on the total absence of navigational aids for ships entering the harbour as had been the case before. However, the light, though sited on a good elevation, was of low intensity and was a mile or so distant from the bar entrance.

It became increasingly evident that what was really needed was a properly constructed lighthouse on the Point. But in those impecunious days it was no easy

matter to find the money for such an expensive undertaking. Thus it was not until May of 1816 that plans and specifications, prepared by Alexander McBride, were in hand and tenders for construction solicited.[4] The successful bid was submitted by contractor James Wood.

All was in readiness for the laying of the cornerstone on the second day of October 1816. The honour of laying this first stone was accorded to the masons, an influential group, well acquainted with ceremony and protocol. In the early afternoon of the appointed day, two lodges gathered at their usual meeting places. Number 242 then marched from the masons' lodge room on Shirley Street to the house occupied by Number 298 on the waterside. From there they embarked in boats and, preceded by a number of other boats all bedecked with flags and bunting, proceeded across the harbour to the site.

The officiating officer explained the business of the day, accepted a plan of the intended building from the architect, along with a set of mason's tools that had been specially made for the ceremony. The following prayer was then read:

Almighty God, Great Architect of the Universe, who by Thy mighty word did speak into Being the numberless Grand Lights of Thy high vaulted firmament! Grant, we humbly beseech Thee, Thy blessing on the undertaking now before us, vouchsafe that the Beacon, whose Foundations are this day laid in Thy name, may fulfil the just hopes of the founders, that, with Thy aid, it may prove an unerring guide to the benighted Mariner and a lasting and useful monument of public munificence, and as the flame, to burn on this lasting column, will lead the storm-beaten vessel from darkness, peril and alarm, into the port of security, so may the Light of Thy word, oh Lord, be a beacon to us all, to guide us from the dark and troubled sea of this life: into the bright and peaceful harbour of Thine Eternal Grace and Glory in the world to come. And this we humbly pray in the name of Thy only Son, Christ Jesus the Redeemer.

After the three elements of consecration were sanctified, the brethren moved to the east side of the foundation where, with the usual solemnities, a prepared stone was raised, then lowered and adjusted into place. This done, there were a few more short speeches and ceremonies, followed by some stirring renditions by the military band of His Majesty's 2nd West India Regiment. The grand finale was a discharge of artillery at Hog Island Point, 'consisting of three times 3 guns'. This salvo was answered by an equal number of guns from the ramparts of Fort Charlotte.

The guests then retired to a nearby house where they enjoyed an excellent collation with the compliments of the contractor. The waves in the harbour were running a little high that day and as a consequence a number of the invited ladies decided not to make the crossing. Apart from this, the proceedings all went well.

A further interesting note is that prior to the laying of the cornerstone, a cavity had been dug into the bedrock and into this hole a phial had been deposited and cemented. The phial contained, and still does, we suppose, 'a small collection of coins and medals, with a legend recording the date and other more important incidents of the commencement of the structure'.

The stones for the tower were quarried nearby, not far from the keeper's dwelling. The quarry which was left trim and neat can still be seen. The limestone tower took nearly a year to build. But on the evening of 1 September 1817, everything was in readiness, including

a lantern of octagonal form, imported from England, and the light was exhibited for the first time.[5]

The stone tower has weathered many a storm. During the 1866 hurricane the ocean rolled completely over Hog Island into the harbour in surges so enormous that the crests of the waves were level with the gallery of the lighthouse, 60 feet above the sea. Governor Rawson reported, 'The lantern of the Hog Island lighthouse was broken and most of the lamps and reflectors destroyed or seriously damaged'.[6]

In April of 1931 the light was semi-automated and the keeper was retired on a pension of £120 a year.[7] The last man to hold the post of keeper of the kerosene-fuelled light was John Drudge, known to his friends as 'the Admiral'.[8] For 37 years he had been at the bar, keeping the light and attending to a number of other duties. At the time of retirement he told of some of his experiences: of shipwrecks and cries for help during dark and stormy nights and of his own efforts to save those who were 'in peril on the sea'. A particularly harrowing story concerned an assistant keeper who lived alone in his own little house. During a storm the sea began to smash against the house and the frightened man tried to make his way to the keeper's house. As soon as he was in the open, a billow rolled right over the island, taking both the assistant keeper and his home with it. Drudge, however, managed to save the man from drowning as he had saved others before and after. 'The Admiral' did his job well. 'During the many rages, storms and hurricanes which had howled at the bar he was steadfast at his post in the lantern room of the lighthouse.'

Apparently, after Drudge retired, it was found that a keeper was still needed for turning on and off the gas cylinder and hoisting the flags. Egbert Hall filled this job until 1948 at which time it was taken over by Eugene Hall. By 1958 the light was completely automated and keepers became redundant.

The lighthouse was neglected for many years and despite an occasional coat of paint is still a sorry sight. The curious walk through it at will, as if they were exploring an old castle. The light on the familiar old sentinal is not completely extinguished but it is too weak to send its beams across the waves. Its flashes are of such a low luminosity as to seem tired and about to

The lighthouse on Paradise (Hog) Island.

expire. Furthermore the flagstaff, to which keepers used to pay such assiduous attention, is bare these days. The national flag is never seen at the masthead and storm warning signals are never hoisted. The keeper's house, once a charming bungalow, is now weather-beaten and dilapidated. Surely this complex, the signpost of the Port of Nassau, deserves better treatment.

Before leaving the lighthouse area, there is also the story of an unusual experiment in salt making in the nineteenth century. The American physician, whom we met earlier in connection with a 'maroon' to the deserted barracks, made a visit to the island in 1823 to see some salt pans.[9] These pans were located near the lighthouse and were based on an unusual conception, being cut out of the solid limestone rock. Owned by a Mr Seton of New York, the pans were designed to produce salt by the usual local process of solar evaporation. The experiment did not work and the reasons for failure, according to the owner, were that 'the water was not saline enough' and 'the coral rock too porous'. We would guess that the latter reason alone was sufficient to guarantee failure for salt had been produced at nearby Rose Island for more than a hundred years utilising sea water of the same salinity.

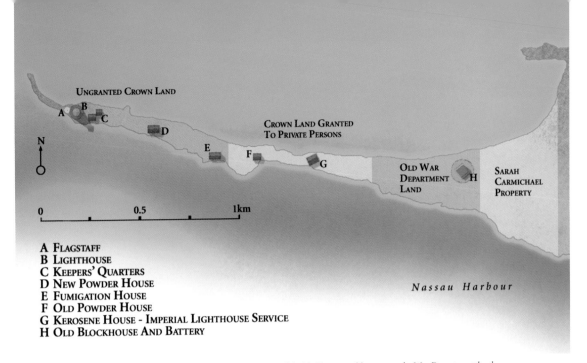

UNGRANTED CROWN LAND

CROWN LAND GRANTED TO PRIVATE PERSONS

OLD WAR DEPARTMENT LAND

SARAH CARMICHAEL PROPERTY

N

0   0.5   1km

Nassau Harbour

A FLAGSTAFF
B LIGHTHOUSE
C KEEPERS' QUARTERS
D NEW POWDER HOUSE
E FUMIGATION HOUSE
F OLD POWDER HOUSE
G KEROSENE HOUSE - IMPERIAL LIGHTHOUSE SERVICE
H OLD BLOCKHOUSE AND BATTERY

Western end of Hog Island showing structures on the Crown land and site of the blockhouse and battery on the War Department land.

Separated by wide distances from the lighthouse and from each other, were four small buildings on the harbour side of that rocky coast. Each stood alone as if there was some reason for its solitude.

Farthest east was the Old Powder House, which was built specifically for the storage and safekeeping of gunpowder. Prior to its construction, powder had been stored in any convenient place in the city in private houses, cellars and stores. It was long feared that a bolt of lightning, fire or other accident, might ignite a barrel or two, start a chain reaction and blow up the town. A notice, published in 1828, informed the public that 'the merchants' powder house on Hog Island is now finished and ready for use'.[10] An area of Crown land on which the Powder House was located was sold to private interests in 1939 and the Assembly voted £500 for the construction of the New Powder House further to the west.[11] In very recent years yet another house, called the Dynamite House, was built in the Pine Barrens, New Providence.

In response to pleas from ship owners and insurance companies, and to the dismay of Bahamian wreckers, the Imperial Government constructed a number of lighthouses throughout The Bahamas between 1836 and the late 1870s.[12] To fuel these lights, kerosene had to be imported in fairly large quantities. A special building, locally known as the Kerosene House, was constructed on Hog Island for the storage of the flammable liquid.

The Fumigating House was built in the early 1930s.[13] This was designed to rid the luggage and belongings of incoming passengers of vermin and disease-carrying germs.

These four houses outlived their usefulness. Two of them, the Old Powder House and the Kerosene House, are incorporated into private homes and only their southern facades can be seen. The Fumigating House and the New Powder House, both in a state of disrepair, still stand alone as relics of a bygone age.

In the late 1930s a substantial portion of this Crown land was sold to private investors. At present only 21 acres at the extreme western tip remain ungranted.[14]

8
Shipyards and Dockyards

Since the beginning of New Providence's history we may suppose that the harbour shore of Hog Island has been used for the careening and overhauling of vessels. But there was nothing singular about that as the same sort of work could be done, and was done, on many sites throughout The Bahamas. Furthermore, it was customary in those days for the crews themselves to take care of all matters relating to the refitting of their vessels.

It was not until about 1788 that a regular shipyard was established on Hog Island.[1] And from that year until fairly recent times, the island has been the dockyard of The Bahamas.

As noted in an earlier chapter, John Russell was granted 300 acres on Hog Island by Dunmore in 1789 but he may have already been established there prior to this date.[2] He had been a shipbuilder at St John's, East Florida, and when he moved to The Bahamas he came in a brig of his own building, the *Live Oak.*[3] He brought along all of his tools and equipment and finding a good place for careening boats on Hog Island, he established a shipyard there.

Dr Thelma Peters, who is a great student of Bahamian Loyalists, gives a good insight into some of Russell's activities. She writes:

Not only did The Bahamas offer a superior quality of timber for boat building, but any ship built in The Bahamas had the privilege of British registry.

That Russell prospered is evident by the number of times he loaned money to other Loyalists, usually with slaves for security. When Thomas Armstrong failed as an Abaco planter, Russell took him into the partnership of a large Plantation in the Caicos Islands.

When Russell heard of slaves, trained in ship-building, being offered for sale, he bought them. That Russell had still another side interest is suggested by an advertisement which he placed in the Bahama Gazette *for June 20, 1789, in which he offered for sale 'Twenty Prime Young New Negroes – Mostly boys', together*

with some cypress and cedar shingles, also some masts and spars.[4]

In May of 1791 Lord Dunmore placed a notice in the *Bahama Gazette* warning trespassers and poachers to stay off Hog Island. He claimed to be the proprietor of the entire island 'except 30 acres belonging to Mr Russell the shipbuilder'.[5] It is not known how Russell's estate, which a few years before had been 300 acres came to be reduced to 30 acres. However, a month later, Russell offered his property, the shipyard and 30 acres of land, for sale or lease.[6] This is difficult to understand since he seemed to have been doing so well. Whether the property passed into other hands then, or later, we do not know. But we do know that the shipyard carried on.

Some idea of the quality of workmanship can be gained from an article which appeared in the *Royal Gazette* on 11 February 1829:

On Saturday, His Majesty's Schooner Speedwell *was launched from the Shipyard at Hog Island where she had been rebuilt…*[7] *This vessel is said to be about 180 tons burden, constructed entirely of the timber and planks of these islands, and is considered by people who have built vessels here, to be superior in every respect to any ever launched in this colony. She is of a beautiful model and is said to be as neatly and strongly put together as wood and copper can be anywhere.*

The Royal Victoria Hotel was built in Nassau by two American contractors, J S Howell and a co-partner. It was finished in 1861. It seems that Howell soon after coming to The Bahamas became attracted to Hog Island. He bought the property granted to Sarah Carmichael by Dunmore in 1789, named it Howelton and built a fine residence near the north beach.[8]

The same year that the Royal Victoria was finished, the American Civil War commenced.

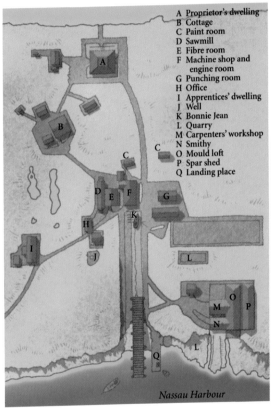

A	Proprietor's dwelling
B	Cottage
C	Paint room
D	Sawmill
E	Fibre room
F	Machine shop and engine room
G	Punching room
H	Office
I	Apprentices' dwelling
J	Well
K	Bonnie Jean
L	Quarry
M	Carpenters' workshop
N	Smithy
O	Mould loft
P	Spar shed
Q	Landing place

Nassau Harbour

Howell's dockyard at Hog Island during the American Civil War.

A week after the outbreak of hostilities, President Lincoln proclaimed a sea blockade of the Confederacy and getting contraband into the Southern States became a dangerous but rewarding enterprise. Blockade runners, because of hard usage and the accidents to which they were prone, frequently required repairs, and Howell saw in this the opportunity for a dockyard business. After all, he already had a piece of property

which was suitable for that purpose. He built a slipway or a marine railway on the harbour side and it seems that the operation prospered throughout the war.[9] It must have been a fairly large facility for many of the blockade runners were of 500 tons or more.

Blockade runner aground on north side of Hog Island, near the lighthouse, during the American Civil War.

While on the subject of blockade runners, the fate of one in particular is relevant to this story. On the north shore of Hog Island, near the lighthouse, can be seen the rusty remains of a steel ship which went ashore there during the Civil War. This ship, which has defied all attempts by the curious to discover its name, left Nassau harbour with a load of contraband, destined for a Confederate port.[10] As was customary, she navigated a circuitous route so as to minimise the chances of detection. She gained the open Atlantic by way of the North-east Providence Channel using the Hole-in-the-Wall light as a guide. After clearing The Bahamas, however, she was set upon by some Federal men-of-war which were on the watch. It must have been a harrowing night for the captain and crew of that blockade runner, keeping a full head of steam to obtain maximum speed, dodging to port and starboard in frantic efforts to shake off their determined pursuers, and all the while trying to make it to the south-west and the safety of Nassau harbour. During the hours of hectic manoeuvring to escape the Federal guns, the pilots must have lost all sense of the ship's exact position. But while they were trying to determine this, they saw a light which they took to be their old friend, the Hole-in-the-Wall. The ship was veered slightly to port so as to keep clear of the rocky headland and soon after that she ran aground. It transpired that they were 40 miles further to the south-west than they had thought and the light they took to be the Hole-in-the-Wall was in fact the Hog Island light. There is still enough left of the ship to constitute a prominent monument to that fatal mistake.

The remains of a blockade runner.

During the Civil War, Hog Island was not only the dockyard of The Bahamas, but the coaling station as well. A writer, after expressing the wish that the name of the island were changed, went on to describe the bustling activity of Hog Island in the coaling business. He mentioned four locations which were supplying the 'black diamonds' to blockade runners: the depot of Messrs Sawyer and Menendez; that of Messrs Saunders and Son, where 6,000 tons were deposited; the extensive depot of Messrs George Chambers and Company; and that of George Preston which, though mentioned last, was decidedly not the least among the newly established depots, being able to store 50,000 tons.[11]

'Since the termination of the war all is dullness and depression',[12] according to a contemporary writer. And no doubt the dockyard, like all other businesses, fell on bad days after peace was declared in 1865.

In December 1872 Howell died at his beach residence on Hog Island, and 15 months later the dry dock

George Higgs' house and harbour.

property was sold at auction to Messrs G W Higgs and company for £2,350.[13] These gentlemen let it be known that they intended to carry on the business of the dry dock themselves. And this they did for 17 years, at the end of which time a catastrophe intervened.

During the afternoon of 18 June 1889, dense volumes of smoke were seen to be issuing from Hog Island.[14] The dockyard was on fire. A number of people soon made their way across the harbour to try to render assistance in fighting the flames.

The fire which had started in a small building was attributed to the upsetting of a small stove which was being used for the purpose of heating irons employed in soldering some leaking petroleum tins. The fire quickly spread to the main building which contained 2,000 cases of petroleum recently salvaged from a wreck at Grand Bahama. Two fire engines were taken from Nassau, one on a raft which capsized and the other on a dredger which got safely across. But the fire could not be contained. It raged until the entire shore facilities of the dockyard had been consumed.

The loss to Mr Higgs was estimated to be £3,000, 'the heaviest loss ever sustained by any one man in the colony by the destructive element of fire'.

The Marine Railway and Dry Docking Plant at Howelton was leased by Mr Higgs to Messrs Brice and Ranger in 1901.[15] These gentlemen owned a general store and were active in the sponge industry by way of providing vessels and supplies.

This new venture was not looked upon as a complement to their sponging interests, for the dock was not designed to handle small vessels. The railway was seen as 'a valuable adjunct to the shipping facilities of the port, and its restoration to the former condition will, we think, be of great advantage, not only to the large vessels owned in the colony, but also to the foreign shipping that might put into Nassau and require repairs.'[16]

The renovated facility, renamed the Nassau Marine Railway, was pronounced ready for use on 3 January 1903. In that same year, the lighthouse tender, *Richmond*, was hauled out. It was noted that it had been 'a long time since a vessel of the size of the *Richmond* (650 tons) has been taken up on this dock'.[17] And it was proudly stated that the dry dock was capable of handling any vessel that could enter the harbour.

While the Nassau Marine Railway business was moving ahead full steam in the dry docking and repairs of large vessels, a new facility for the accommodation of smaller craft was built further to the west. This marine railway was constructed by Hilton C Albury on the property he had bought from the War Department.

In August of 1905 '17 schooners and boats of various sizes were hauled up there', and 30 or 40 others were waiting their turn.[18] This dock must have filled a great local need. Two years later 35 craft were hauled out including 'five locally owned sailing yachts, and 16

Nassau Boat Works.

schooners and six sloops generally employed in sponging'.[19]

The dock experienced a decade or more of prosperity, but in 1923 'the yard had but one small slip and was not very ambitious in its output.[20] If the dock was not very ambitious, a young man, R T Symonette, was ambitious to an extraordinary degree. After careful consideration, he bought it.

About three years prior to this purchase, Symonette had been made the local agent for the Bahamas Gulf Oil Company.[21] This company installed the first bulk storage facility for petroleum products in The Bahamas, situated on Hog Island near the Nassau Boat Works. Thus, for a few years he was able to observe the day-to-day workings of that small dockyard and to give much thought as to what he could make of it.

When he did finally purchase the boat works he engaged the services of A R Braynen as manager of the Gulf Oil depot so that he could turn his full attention to the dockyard.

It is interesting that these two men, from the same small settlement, and related by blood, both became prominent in the business and political life of The Bahamas. Symonette was later knighted and became the first Premier of The Bahamas. Braynen also received a knighthood, became Speaker of the House of Assembly and the first Bahamian High Commissioner to the United Kingdom.

As to the Gulf Oil Company, in 1930 it was bought by the West India Oil Company. West India continued the same kind of operation on Hog Island for more than 20 years when it transferred its bulk storage operation, under the name of Esso, to Clifton Pier on the south-west coast of New Providence.

Symonette had purchased the Nassau Boat Works and four acres of land. And on the first day of January 1924, he began the building of a shipyard, 'which will be far more efficient and modern than anything the colony has had before'.[22] The prospective complex was named the R T Symonette Shipyards Ltd.

The necessary materials for the new dockyard were bought in Jacksonville and transported to Hog Island in one of Symonette's own vessels, the three-masted *Alma R*.[23] When completed, the $200,000 shipyard was equipped with three marine railways: one for small

Sir Roland T Symonette.

boats, one for vessels up to 300 tons and the third for ships up to 1,500 tons.[24] The machine shop opened on to a pier on which a track ran down to a T-headed wharf, 300 feet long and 40 feet wide.[25] This wharf had a water depth of 22 feet at low tide, and could take vessels which formerly had to lie in the stream. Every tool and facility for the dry docking, repair and building of boats was there. And everything was electrically operated.

Bahamas Gulf Oil Company's storage facilities and the adjacent R T Symonette Shipyards Ltd.

Dry dock at the Symonette Shipyard.

The names of some of the vessels hauled out at the dock were *Richmond, Firebird, Miami, Coloma, William C Bickle, Nassauvian, Priscilla, Sarah E Douglas, Louise F, Ballymena* and the three-masted lumber-carrying fleets of Harbour Island and Abaco.

The Symonette Shipyard on Hog Island served The Bahamas well for 14 years. In 1938 the operation was moved to the Nassau waterfront.[26] Up until the early 1980s there was a small boat works on Paradise Island to the west of the bridge. It seemed to maintain, in a small way, the continuity of shipbuilding and ship repairing which had played such a long and interesting role in the island's history.

An interesting story concerning Symonette comes to us from the year 1924, when he was engaged in his mammoth shipyard project.[27] The yard's communications with Nassau were maintained by two motor launches, and he must have often suffered from delays in bringing to the site urgently needed material. Fernley Rae, a pioneer in real estate, had suggested that Hog Island should be linked to Nassau by a causeway from Malcolm's Park via Potter's Cay. Asked what he thought of the suggestion, Symonette had said, 'It was a capital idea, which would make Hog Island a beautiful tourist resort, the equal of Miami Beach, if the developments were properly controlled; there was no doubt about that'.

9

Agriculture, Bathing Houses and Amusement Centres

*U*p to the time of the Loyalists, Hog Island had been used by the people of New Providence as a common. Small plots were cleared for farming and livestock was raised there. Lord Dunmore was not interested in contributing to the continuance of these peasant pursuits. His object was to get Loyalists on the land, with retinues of slaves who could produce money-making plantations. That is why, except for the land set aside for government use, the island was divided into only four allotments.

The records do not reveal much about the island during the plantation period. That is probably because it was overshadowed by the activity that was going on in the cotton islands of the south-east Bahamas. Nevertheless, there is no reason to believe that Hog Island was not caught up in the cotton fever which spread to wherever the crop could be grown.

Governor Rawson wrote in 1867 that 'the few plantations and dwellings which existed on the island in the time of slavery have been almost all abandoned'.[1]

During the latter part of the nineteenth century, the pineapples and sisal industries became the dominant agricultural pursuits of the colony. And here again Hog Island was involved. A newspaper article in 1871 describes the increase of cultivation taking place in New Providence and goes on to say:

At Howelton too, on the north side of the harbour, a pinary is being laid out by the enterprising proprietor of the Dry Dock, who has also a considerable portion of land allotted to the coconut plantation. The pitre – sisal plant – has been thoroughly established on the estate, and thickly lines the avenue leading from the dock to the dwelling house.[2]

We may assume that much of the rest of the suitable land of the island was planted out in pineapples and sisal.

Citrus fruit had been grown in The Bahamas since the islands were first settled. However, this industry received a shot in the arm because of the 'Great Freeze' of 1894–5, when great damage was done to the Florida citrus groves, located in the middle of the state.[3] Bahamians and foreign entrepreneurs reasoned that the frost-free Bahamas would be a better place for the growing of citrus fruit and the United States would provide a ready market as it had done before Florida entered the picture. Citrus did not prove to be the bonanza that had been anticipated, for a number of reasons. But, nevertheless, the groves were there well after the turn of the century to brighten the landscape.

Mr G W Higgs, who had bought Howelton, had the misfortune of having the dockyard destroyed by fire, as noted in the previous chapter; but the house near the north side, which Howell had built, was saved. Between the dock site and the house Higgs too developed a citrus orchard where its previous owner had planted pineapples and sisal.

Hog Island has always held a fascination for pleasure seekers. The fine beaches of the north side, especially, have exerted a magnet-like attraction to generations of Bahamians and visitors. We saw that before the year 1788 there was a 'Banqueting House' on the island. Going to that place was something of a 'maroon'; an opportunity to escape the torpid atmosphere of Nassau and to enjoy the invigorating and unspoiled surroundings. But there were few who ventured into the sea in those days. Sea bathing was thought by most adults to be both unwholesome and dangerous, and only the young and daring would enter beyond standing depth and a sure footing. By the 1890s habits had changed considerably and swimming moved to the fore as the most alluring pleasure that the island had to offer. A consequence of this was the building of 'bathing houses'.

William Benedict Reilly, a visitor and writer who came this way (around 1895) was overwhelmed with the charm of Hog Island beaches and the sea water which washes them.[4] He wrote:

On the north side of the island, is about one mile of the most magnificent beach in the world, with its sands white as chalk and soft as velvet. There is an ideal surf which must be seen to be appreciated. The water during the winter season is sufficiently cool to be invigorating and bracing, but never cool enough to be other than grateful to the most delicate constitution. The surf rolls at times at a great height, but there is never any undertow, and the descent of the bottom is such that any depth desirable may be had within a distance of twenty-five or thirty feet from the shore.

One of the delights of sea bathing at Hog Island, as described by the writer, was that a bather could dive under water and 'see about him for an incredibly long distance in any direction... The island is covered with oranges, cocoanuts, and all tropical fruits which visitors may feast upon to their heart's content for a trifling consideration'.

Mr E L Moore, a Nassau businessman, had built a 'pretty summer house' on a high peak overlooking both the harbour and the ocean. During the winter season this house was converted into a bathing house. For one shilling sterling (24 cents), a visitor could obtain a ride across the harbour on boats which left Nassau every hour, enjoy a swim, with a changing room and bathing suit supplied, and feast on succulent fruit. Reilly pointed out that there were other bathing houses on Hog Island, 'but none which for convenience and perfect appointments for bathing

in comfort and safety, bear any comparison with this'.[5]

Two other bathing houses might be mentioned which existed at that time or a few years later: the Higgs' house, which had been built by Howell on the dry dock property and Hilton Albury's house which stood on the site of the old blockhouse and battery. The latter, called the Mound, was the rendezvous of boys who enjoyed swimming in the nude. 'Since the Mound was some distance from the other bathing areas, objections to nudity there seem to have been very few'. However, as late as 1923 a sharp protest was lodged in a letter to the *Guardian*. 'I am told', wrote the correspondent, 'that there is a serious complaint that people are forming a habit of bathing over at Hog Island without troubling about bathing costumes. Now this Arcadian simplicity may be all very well on a desert island, but it is not very pleasant for the keepers of the lighthouse and their families'.[6] He suggested that it might be necessary to send a policeman over there to stop the practice.

The Higgs' house (formerly Howelton) and picnickers on the North Beach (Paradise Beach), around 1900.

These establishments followed the *modus operandi* of the Moore house: the owners used them as a summer house and during the winter months they served as bathing houses; transportation was provided; there were facilities for changing, swimsuits supplied, and always the inevitable fresh fruit. And the price for the package was pretty constant at about one shilling per person.

Ladies eating oranges on skewers.

Oranges, picked fresh from the trees, were peeled and served on skewers. Free things have an unusual attraction and 'all one can eat' was bound to produce some amusing anecdotes. One of them which has survived concerns an American visitor who ate between 30 and 40 oranges.[7] Maybe his conscience bothered him and he turned to the old fellow who ran the place and said: 'Guess I'm eating too much, eh?' 'Oh no', replied the old chap. 'Ain't dis island name Hawg?'

The multiplicity of bathing houses resulted in competition among the proprietors. Many advertisements are thus to be found in contemporary numbers of the *Guardian* extolling the superiority of one in particular over the others. It became clear, however, that true superiority could only be gained by increasing the attractions. Consequently, in January of 1898 we hear of something new and different.

Mr J L Saunders, a prominent businessman of Nassau, had built a pleasure resort on the western part of the island in 1897, which he named the Casino.

It was not a casino in the modern sense of the word but, as described in the quaint phraseology of the day: 'a veritable amusement paradise, where energy and enterprise have created a modern garden of Hesperides'.[8] The aim of the proprietor was to provide an up-to-date pleasure resort in connection with the city, 'where visitors and other pleasure seekers would be able to spend a quiet hour in complete enjoyment'.[9]

On the day of the grand opening in January of 1898, 'the site was gaily adorned with bunting, and when the bands of music arrived on the scene, merriment naturally increased'.[10] The day was evidently regarded as a holiday in Nassau and Mr Saunders estimated that 4,000 persons crossed the harbour in a steam yacht and several steam launches to enjoy the festivities.

At the Casino various types of amusement brightened the afternoon and evening. There was dining and dancing, bowling and billiards, and fireworks after dark. On the beach, besides the usual swimming and frolicking, there was a bicycle race which created great excitement. The weather was beautiful and it was not until the small hours of the next morning that everybody had returned to Nassau. Subsequent advertisements draw attention to bi-weekly picnics at the Casino, to boat races, foot races, sack races, agricultural contests and candy-pulls.

Fire struck the Casino during the early morning of 21 December 1900. The main buildings were destroyed, but fortunately they were covered by insurance. The very next year the establishment was back in business again.

The fourth of July, American Independence Day, was celebrated there, and a ventriloquist act was performed under the patronage of the Governor, Sir William Carter. Trapeze performances, and tight and slack wire performances were regularly featured. A note of discord was, however, sounded in a revealing letter to the editor of the *Guardian*. Difficulties were being experienced because of a clique which frequented the bar room and spoiled the pleasure of others. The writer states that

'when liquor is in, wit is out', and recommended that two policemen be assigned to the area to keep order.[11]

Sometime prior to 1900, James P Sands (later Sir James P Sands), a Nassau merchant dealing in groceries and lumber, acquired an acreage on Hog Island which was developed along the same lines as the Casino. He named his estate the Saratoga, probably after a Ward Line Steamer which then brought visitors from New York to Nassau. The Casino and the Saratoga were the amusement centres of the New Providence area for some years and they engaged in fierce competition with each other in the attractions they offered.

Sands' property included that most beautiful crescent of the Hog Island beach and this too was given the name of the Saratoga. A newspaper article of January 1900 stated that it was the object of the manager, Mr L Wolfe, 'to make a first class family pleasure resort, a resort where you can take your wife,

North Beach 1904.

mother, sister or children without any fear of encountering anything that is not of the utmost respectability. The manager will see strictly to the stopping of any questionable characters from landing at the Saratoga'.[12]

The normal hours of opening were every evening from 7.00 p.m. until 12.00 p.m. Attractions were obtained through a theatrical agent in New York. They included high-wire walkers, trick-bicycle riders, and aerial performers of all descriptions. Attention was also drawn to a new and beautiful bathing house, '90 feet long

Postcard of Hotel Colonial 1922.

and every convenience for surf bathing on one of the finest parts of the beach on the island'.[13] Dancing classes were held three days a week at a cost of $5.00 for 12 lessons. There was a guarantee attached to these lessons: if a student did not learn 'the Waltz and two-step' within the prescribed period, his money was refunded.[14] On Friday afternoons from 2.00 to 7.00 p.m. children and their escorts were admitted free of cost. They enjoyed a ride across the harbour and dancing at the Pavilion. A theatrical troupe gave performances at the Saratoga Theatre on Monday and Thursday evenings and on Friday afternoons, a matinee for ladies and children.[15] Much to the delight and satisfaction of the patrons, vaudeville shows were put on four nights a week. Admission was two shillings or 48 cents.

It would appear that perhaps Sands had been too

ambitious with his enterprise. The money expended on managers and imported entertainment groups was probably more than the operation could bear. Ten years after the flurry of activities which characterised the beginning we hear of another winter season opening of the Saratoga. Nothing grand or exceptional was offered then – sea bathing – fruit lunch – fresh water shower baths – one shilling (24 cents) per person. Bathing suits were not supplied. The advertisement was not signed by a manager but by Jas P Sands himself.[16] This sounds much like a reversion to the bathing houses of the 1890s.

The Hotel Colonial was built by H M Flagler in Nassau in 1901 and it soon vied with the Hog Island amusement centres for the tourist dollars. And slowly, but surely, the centre of amusement activity shifted to Nassau.

In 1922, however, the Hotel Colonial, being a wooden structure, was completely destroyed by fire. At this point in time an American, Frank Munson, entered the tourist picture. He obtained a loan of £430,000 from the Bahamas Government for building a new hotel and operating it for ten years.[17] A further £15,000 was loaned to a subsidiary company for the construction of a golf course to the west of Nassau which, with subsequent improvements, is still in use.

Tennis courts at the Hotel Colonial.

Meanwhile, back in 1917 the old Ward Line, which had performed the vital steamship service between New York and Nassau since 1879, refused to renew its contract with the Bahamas Government.[18] Ships were found to fill in here and there, but the irregular service was far from satisfactory. Munson had married a McCormick whose family owned the McCormick Steamship Line and through this connection he learned something about ships and shipping. Furthermore, his wife had bought the Royal Victoria Hotel so that together, they owned the only two hotels in Nassau. Therefore, the institution of a regular New York–Nassau steamship service was vital to his interests. We suppose he began to see himself as another Flagler, a man who owned both hotels and the means of transporting visitors to occupy them.

In 1921 Munson signed a ten-year contract with the Government to provide a weekly service from January to April and a fortnightly service for the rest of the year at an annual subsidy of £35,000.[19] Three ships, the *Munorleans, Munargo* and *Munamar* comprised the Munson Steamship Line. The *Munorleans* was the largest and the *Munamar* the smallest, but the *Munargo*, which could accommodate 250 passengers, was the most frequent visitor and the best known in Nassau.

It is no exaggeration to say that during the 1920s the tourist industry of The Bahamas was in Munson's hands. In 1983, Mr Charles Hall, Senior, a sprightly octogenarian with a long, clear memory, could look back to half a century of tourist development in Nassau. He worked with the New Yorker during his business life in The Bahamas and was convinced that Munson, more than any other man, deserves the accolade of 'The Father of Modern Bahamian Tourism'.[20]

Munson realised that, in coming to The Bahamas, tourists were looking for something more than a hotel atmosphere, however well appointed and pleasant it might be. They wanted to see something of the tropical paradise which had lured them to this spot. Consequently, he bought a property adjacent to and immediately to the east of Saratoga, which ran from coast to coast. The beach which the property faced had been called, up to that time, Saratoga. He now endowed it with the more attractive name of Paradise Beach, a name which has pertained ever since.

He built a fine wharf on the harbour side and constructed cabanas near the beach for changing rooms and the serving of refreshments.[21] He made no attempt to duplicate the multiple activities of the Saratoga and the Casino, preferring to rely on the natural beauty of the area and the incomparable swimming to be found there.

Between the eastern end of Hog Island and the western end of Athol Island lies the eastern entrance to Nassau harbour, called the Narrows. On the sea bottom of this cut were sea gardens of incredible beauty, much diminished now by human interference.

These gardens had long been recognised as a valuable natural asset because of their attraction to visitors. As far back as 1892 the Government had sought to protect these gardens by an Act of the legislature, which made it an offence to 'remove or take by any means whatsoever, from the bottom of the sea between Hog Island and Athol Island, any coral, sea fan, or other marine product thereon growing, lying or being'. Eight years later the Commandant of Police published a notice reminding the public of this Act.

Munson had two ferries built, the *Gleeful* and the *Joyful*; each capable of accommodating 50 or 60 passengers. These boats were fitted with dry wells, the bottoms of which were formed of glass plates. A group of tourists, seated around the well, could look down and see, quite clearly, the bottom of the sea 20 or more feet below. Tourists were exhilarated by the scene which was revealed to them – a phantasmagoria of colours, shapes and movements. Corals, sea-feathers, gorgonias, sea-fans, sea-urchins, sponges and sea-stars formed a backdrop. Multitudes of fishes, darting here and there, forever on the move, added a lively brilliancy to the scene. The *Gleeful* and *Joyful* made several scheduled trips daily. They displayed prominent signs which read: 'GLASS BOTTOM BOAT, SEA GARDENS FERRY, PARADISE BEACH'.

Passengers on the Munson ships were acquainted with the pleasures to be expected from these excursions while still at sea. Having disembarked, many of them went directly to the ferry boats. They were taken first to view the wonders of the undersea world and then to Paradise Beach harbour wharf. The half-mile walk to the beach was along a path made cool and pleasant by a continuous arch formed of casuarina trees which had been planted on both sides of the roadway. At the end of the walk was Paradise Beach – a dazzling crescent of white coral sand with the iridescent Bahama Sea gently lapping at its edge. It was not unusual for visitors who saw that tropical panorama for the first time, to experience an ecstasy of emotion.

The sand and sea always lived up to expectations. At the changing cabanas which had been erected on the high ground adjacent to the beach, the visitors quickly kicked off their shoes and put on swim suits; they walked the beach and enjoyed the pleasant sensation of the fine textured sand beneath their bare feet; they swam in sea water of unequalled clarity and between these

activities, refreshing drinks and delightful snacks were enjoyed. On returning to ship or hotel they really had the feeling that they had tasted a bit of Paradise. Back home they talked of their thrilling experiences and 'Paradise Beach' became well-known throughout the United States.

When the *Munargo* first began visiting Nassau, she had to anchor outside the bar and passengers were ferried ashore on tenders. Munson persuaded the Bahamas Government to deepen the channel and in 1928 the ship entered the harbour and berthed at Prince George Wharf for the first time.[22] This was an important advance in the convenience and comfort of tourists, and therefore an asset to the tourist industry.

1920s bathing suits on Paradise Beach.

Paradise Beach, much as it was in Frank Munson's time.

Soon after that, however, the chill winds of depression were blowing through the homes and businesses of America. Fewer people were inclined to spend money on travel and Munson's Steamship Lines began to feel the pinch of economic troubles. What Munson needed at that time was an increase in the subsidy.

But the Bahamas Government, after the bootlegging boom, was also in financial difficulties, and when the steamship contract came up for renewal it could only offer one half of the original £35,000 which had been paid during the previous ten years.[23] Munson accepted it but soon went broke. He retired to his native New York and some years later was killed in an automobile accident. His steamships were sold by his estate to the United Fruit Company which performed a less satisfactory service between New York and Nassau for a number of years.[24] The Spanish Wells people took over the 'glass bottom boat and ferry' business and Paradise Beach carried on as before.

10
The Western End

A long the western boundary of Saratoga, a line may be drawn which will divide Hog Island into two unequal parts. The island to the west of that line is referred to as the 'western end'. And since the course of development of this area has been different to the rest of the island, it deserves separate treatment.

During the early years of this century, a few Americans became attracted to Hog Island and the Hilton Albury estate, in particular, as a site for their winter homes. Among these pioneers were Mr and Mrs George Bullock, Mr and Mrs Irving Cox, Mr and Mrs R Agassiz and Mrs Eliot Bacon.[1] This group created a 'settlement' with a 'cottage' atmosphere. Sometimes it was referred to as the 'American colony'.

Mr George Bullock was looked upon as the doyen of this American winter colony.[2] One day a fellow colonist said to him, 'Why don't we get up a little club of our own?'[3] Bullock offered to sublease for $1 a year a portion of the property he himself had leased. A visiting architect volunteered to draw the plans. The Porcupine Club was organised early in 1912 and the clubhouse opened to its charter members in January 1913. We can find no explanation as to why the name Porcupine was chosen. We can assume that it was because of the animal's rough resemblance to a hog. And like members of the club, it was foreign to Hog Island.

The clubhouse, with some enlargement, served its purpose for 16 years and in February 1929 a new building, built by the Turtle Construction Company, a little further to the east, was ready for occupancy.[4]

Throughout its history, the club has been exclusive and small. The original 11 members were increased by 25 in the course of time, and in 1930 members numbered 50.[5] It would seem that there were two main qualifications for membership: one had to be American and very rich. By 'very rich' we do not mean owning just a million dollars or so, but many millions of dollars.

Occasionally, but very occasionally, the American qualification was set aside. The first non-American to be admitted was Lady Williams-Taylor of Montreal.[6]

From the building of the new clubhouse until the beginning of World War II, the Porcupine was the elite rendezvous of prominent Americans. Some members arrived in magnificent yachts which formed a pretty sight against the Hog Island background. There were the *Orion, Vagabond, Corsair, Oceanic, Moby Dick, Atlantic, Crusader, Cutty Sark* and many others. And the owners read like a *Who's Who* in American banking and industry: Fleichmann, Andrew Mellon, J P Morgan, Howard Hughes, Fred Fisher, Vincent Astor and so on.[7]

After the war, the Porcupine Club was soon seen to have been yet another casualty. Many of the old members had died off and there was a general lack of enthusiasm as regards reorganising it again. Most of the remaining members joined the Lyford Cay Club and the land and clubhouse were sold to Porcupine Holdings. Frank Lloyd, the principal of this company also bought the Phillip Gossler estate and that of Arthur Vining Davis. These three properties, comprising 30 acres, were a choice piece of real estate.

The new owner proposed to the proprietors of Club Mediterranée that his property would be a good site for one of their establishments. A contract was made and on 10 December 1977, the 76th member of that company's resort-village organisation opened its doors to the world.

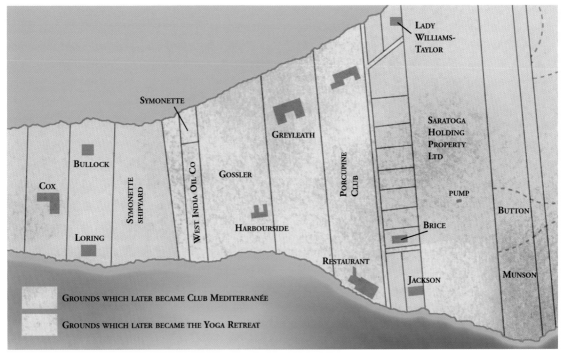

Property of Club Méditerranée and the Yoga Retreat, superimposed on old estates as of 1934.

Club Méditerranée, usually referred to as 'Club Med', was the brain-child of an ex-Olympic Games champion, Gerald Blitz. In 1950 he 'dreamed of a sports oriented vacation centre where city dwellers could exchange their urban pressures and problems for a special place to enjoy the beauties of nature and a completely informal lifestyle, free of daily cares'. That summer in 1950, Club Méditerranée was born at Majorca, Spain, in a tent village. This venture was a success and the revolutionary concept inspired duplication in other countries. In 1983, there were over 100 villages in 26 different countries throughout the world, making Club Med the ninth largest hotel chain with approximately a million guests every year.

The Paradise Island village followed the established pattern. There was some new construction for accommodation purposes, but the old houses were maintained in largely unchanged condition. The lawns and the large trees which enhanced the area were maintained in impeccable order.

The club credited its success to its philosophy of vacationing; a belief that a vacation should be radically different from normal, daily life; a time in the year when 'there were no barriers, rules or restraints, and in which human contacts were made sincerely'. In keeping with this philosophy, the village on Paradise discouraged

Harbour frontage of Club Méditerranée. On the right is the incorporated and renovated Porcupine Club.

fancy wardrobes; there were no telephones, television sets, radios or newspapers to remind guests of the cares of everyday life. The club did have attractive surroundings, however, abundant facilities for sports and recreation, appetising French cuisine and the comradeship of members from many countries and all walks of life.

Members arrived from Nassau by ferry boat or by bus via the bridge. There was always a group to greet them with a song and dance routine. New members quickly changed their city clothes for more informal attire and immediately were conscious of a relaxed atmosphere. They would buy a supply of beads which were put around their necks and used instead of money for all payments in the village.

The club could accommodate 600 guests and employed 300 workers, 200 of whom were Bahamian. Thus it made a real contribution to the Bahamian economy. Its guests were drawn from Club Med members, throughout the world, although non-members were welcome at the normally accepted rate for dinners and shows.

In 1987, the 21-acre village was closed for 26 weeks for renovation, 78 rooms were added and the administrative offices relocated. The existing offices were converted to an upscale restaurant. After 25 years in existence, Club Med on Paradise Island is the busiest in North America. The philosophy has changed somewhat. Singles and honeymooners can still romance there but the facility now welcomes families and teenagers and telephones, television, hairdryers and other amenities have been added.

Immediately to the west of Club Med is a Yoga retreat, but there is no through road to this establishment. It is almost a world unto itself, accessible only by boat from Nassau.

Yoga Retreat.

Mrs Natalie Boswell, daughter of the late H C Albury, inherited a part of the War Department land which her father had bought. And on this beautiful spot she built a charming vacation bungalow. Then at the time of a distressing family situation she met with Swami Vishnu Devananda, a prominent apostle of the Yoga discipline. She studied the principles of Yoga under his guidance and was mentally and spiritually comforted thereby. In appreciation she gave her Hog Island property to Vishnu Devananda on a 99-year lease, to benefit humanity. In 1967 the estate was converted into a Yoga retreat, one of many throughout the world.

In addition to Mrs Boswell's home on the crest of a hill, in the middle of the premises there are a number of small cabins which provide most of the accommodation. When the influx of winter holidaymakers increases to a certain level (over 150), tents have to be erected. And this feature causes the retreat to be referred to sometimes as the 'Tent City'.

Two vegetarian meals are served each day, consisting in part of produce grown in the retreat's own gardens. Meat, fish, eggs, alcohol, tobacco, narcotics and public nudity are forbidden. The daily regimen, which begins with a ringing of the rising bell at 5.30 a.m., would seem austere to the average holidaymaker. But that it is relished by those who have adopted the Yoga way of life,

is evidenced by the fact that most of the guests are annual returnees. The retreat is almost self-sustaining, as guests are invited to assist with work in the kitchen and garden, or wherever they can lend a hand. A wide range of recreational activities is offered and periods of meditation and exercises are a part of the daily routine. In 1983, the retreat complained that noise from its neighbour, Club Med, was disturbing its chantings and meditations. A lawsuit threatened to ensue, but the row was amicably settled when Club Med installed some effective sound barriers.

In January 1993, admirers said goodbye to their founder, 65-year-old, Swami Vishnu Devananda, as he left the Yoga Retreat to be bathed, anointed and die alongside the Ganges. Each year a puja, an ancient Hindu prayer, is chanted in his memory and his teachings of serve, love, give, purify, meditate and realise are still venerated in the retreat he founded 35 years ago.

Apart from Club Med and the Yoga Retreat, there are a number of private homes on this western end, but space does not allow the telling of their histories. Two of these private homes have opened as small hotels. Chaplin House, east of the Yoga Retreat, opened in 1985, offering four bedrooms and a cottage for rent. The Pink House, an old Georgian colonial house near Club Med, opened in 1991, now operates as a four-bedroom hotel.

11
Wenner-Gren

O n 3 September 1939, the first day of World War II, the Athenia, a British passenger liner of 13,500 tons, was outward bound, just west of Ireland. On board were 1,480 passengers and crew. At 9.00 p.m. she was hit by a German torpedo which tore a gaping hole in the hull and she began to sink.[1] But before she went down, the wireless operator was able to tap out a distress signal and details of the stricken ship's position.

Fortunately, the *Southern Cross*, one of the world's largest yachts, was only 50 miles away when the SOS was intercepted. Dr Axel Wenner-Gren, the owner, was on board, making his way to The Bahamas, when the call for assistance came over the wireless. On being notified of the SOS, the captain immediately turned his ship towards the disaster scene at top speed. When it arrived there, the *Athenia* was not to be seen for she had by then gone to the bottom. But the site of the tragedy was well marked by floating wreckage and hundreds of men and women, some huddled in lifeboats, others clinging to the sides of the boats, or just swimming about in the cold Atlantic water.

Boats were quickly lowered from the *Southern Cross* and the rescue began; 378 survivors were brought on board; the remainder were picked up by another vessel which had also responded to the distress call; 112 lives were lost.[2]

The general public was not then inured to the horrors of war as it was later to become. A number of United States citizens had been among the *Athenia's* passengers and the German propaganda machine, anxious to avoid possible adverse American reaction, soon put out a story that it hoped would be believed. It was to the effect that Churchill, himself, had ordered a bomb to be placed on the *Athenia* so that the ship's destruction would poison German–American relations.[3]

Another rumour which made the rounds concerned Dr Axel Wenner-Gren. Because he was known to be closely associated with some prominent German

Passenger smiles in relief after being rescued by the Southern Cross *from the torpedoed* Athenia.

industrialists and political leaders, it was widely believed that he was pro-German. The presence of the *Southern Cross*, so near to the *Athenia* on that fatal night, was interpreted to be more than a coincidence. Perhaps the *Southern Cross* had radioed the position of the *Athenia* to the German submarine command. It is most unlikely that there was any truth in this, but rumours do not need truth to sustain them.

However this may have been, the *Southern Cross* continued its way across the Atlantic, put its cargo of distressed survivors ashore at Miami, and then made for its original destination, the harbour of Nassau. Captain Freddie Brown, Nassau harbour pilot, met the ship a few miles at sea and guided it to its anchorage near Hog Island. He noticed that near the water-line, the normally snow-white sides of the *Southern Cross* were besmirched with oily handprints left by those swimming survivors of the *Athenia* who had desperately tried to grasp something solid in that watery world.

In the sheltered water of Nassau harbour, Wenner-Gren could relax after his harrowing ordeal. From the vantage point of the top deck of the *Southern Cross*, he could enjoy a cool drink while feasting his eyes on the rugged shoreline and tropical foliage of Hog Island, an island which was much on his mind.

Dr Wenner-Gren was one of the world's most successful industrialists. His plants were chiefly located in his native Sweden and in Germany, and his products were sold to all parts of the world. They ranged from vacuum cleaners to refrigerators to Beaufort guns. He was the inventor of the monorail and the tentacles of his investments, which were almost global, embraced mines, power plants, newspapers, shipping and aviation. He was also an economist, yachtsman and author.

In 1937 he had bought the *Southern Cross* from Howard Hughes. The vessel had been built in England by Lord Inchcope seven years before and was originally called the *Rover*. This magnificent yacht was of 3,000 tons displacement and had four decks. She was 322 feet long, 41 feet wide, with a draft of 16 feet. Carrying four lifeboats, the normal crew complement was 40 men.[4]

The Southern Cross *– Wenner-Gren's luxurious yacht.*

Wenner-Gren began a world cruise in October 1937 which lasted for nine months. A year later, he was off again. The vessel journeyed down the east coast of South America, rounded Cape Horn and came to the West Indies by way of the Panama Canal.[5] In Nassau harbour, in March 1939, he told a party of dinner guests that 'he had travelled 70,000 miles or more to all the loveliest spots in the world but had returned to Nassau, and hoped to return often again'.[6]

His yacht was equipped with the finest of radio equipment and all on board were kept informed as the war clouds became more threatening over Europe. By the middle of April 1939 Wenner-Gren was contemplating his return to Sweden. Before leaving he said he hoped to return to Nassau about October to spend the winter here, but 'his movements depended entirely on the European situation'.[7]

Dr Axel Wenner-Gren, the Swede who built his Shangri-La on Hog Island.

Wenner-Gren and Axel Johansson, Engineer, in the engine room of the Southern Cross.

During that same month in 1939 he purchased the Lynch estate at Hog Island for $150,000 and the newspapers reported that 'Mr and Mrs Wenner-Gren, who are on their second visit to Nassau, have decided that it is a delightful place in which to make their winter residence'.[8] The estate included a magnificent house and a splendid, covered tennis court which Lynch had built two years before. Prior to the construction of this estate, all the development on Hog Island had been concentrated at the western end, and those builders who sought beach frontage chose Paradise Beach. Lynch, however, built further to the east and his property fronted on Cabbage Beach.

Edmund C Lynch had had an interesting, early career in industry and banking. Later on in life, he had formed a close friendship with Charles E Merrill which led to the formation of Merrill, Lynch and Company in 1915. This firm was among the first to interest itself in the chain-store industry.[9] Lynch did not have long to enjoy Hog Island. He built there one year and was dead the next.

Wenner-Gren, now having bought his future winter house at Hog Island, left towards the end of April 1939 for his native Sweden. His plan at the time was to return to Hog Island in October or November. However, the imminence of war persuaded him that it would be wise to make an earlier departure, but it was not quite early enough. The outbreak of hostilities found him on the high seas, and he met with the gruesome adventure we have described.

Much was to be made of the fact that he was a close friend of Herman Goering, Vice Marshal of the Third Reich. But, as he always pointed out, he was also a close friend of American presidents and British prime ministers. In cutting a swathe through the industrial world to riches, he had to be farsighted and determined and, no doubt, to some degree, ruthless. Though he always claimed a close attachment to his native Sweden, his industrial activities were probably uppermost in his thoughts, and he assumed a supra-national outlook. With friends, and in convivial surroundings, however, he was most personable and engaging. His stature was commanding – tall, straight and handsome - his full face, topped with a shock of blond hair, displayed honesty and forthrightness.

Like many other businessmen who lead a hurried and hectic life, there came a time when Wenner-Gren sought to find an 'escape hatch'. He must have become familiar with James Hilton's novel *Lost Horizon* in which the author describes a fictitious monastery in the Tibetan Himalayas called Shangri-La. Surrounded by majestic snow-capped peaks, interspersed with fertile valleys, Shangri-La was a Utopia where life approached perfection and people lived to a great age. But Wenner-Gren was too well acquainted with cold climates and mountainous countries to look on that kind of environment as a site for his Utopia, James Hilton notwithstanding. He sought to find his place of peace and contentment among the tropical and subtropical lands of the world. In this pursuit, he travelled far and wide, as we have seen, and finally decided on little Hog Island.

Shangri-La.

Now, in the fall of 1939, he was back at the island of his dreams having left behind a war-maddened Europe. He immediately set to work on remodelling, refurbishing and landscaping his home and grounds and, as might be expected, he named it Shangri-La.

In August of 1940 the Duke of Windsor arrived in Nassau to take up his post as Governor of The Bahamas. He soon discovered that the economic conditions in his island kingdom were in a bad state and getting progressively worse. Tourism, the mainstay of its prosperity, was in a spiralling decline and most of the hotels had closed their doors. Particularly distressing were the thousands of unemployed. The Duke appealed to some wealthy residents of the colony to set some works in motion so as to relieve the situation, and most of them, including Dr Wenner-Gren, responded favourably.

Duke of Windsor and Wenner-Gren watching labourers digging the canal.

At Hog Island there was an inland lake called Burnside's Pond. It was an ugly hole in an otherwise attractive island. The stagnant water was dyed a rusty colour by the sedimentary material which had accumulated there. Margins were overgrown with mangrove trees and saw-grass. A disagreeable smell emanated from the area. Useful only to duck hunters, the pond was a blotch on the landscape. Wenner-Gren put hundreds of men to work on this pond. The silt was cleaned out and the margins bulk-headed. Two canals were cut, one leading to the harbour and one to the north side. An attractive bridge was constructed over each of the canals and boats with short masts and of

An aerial view of Paradise Island before the canal. The Southern Cross *is moored in the harbour.*

An aerial view of Paradise Island circa 1945.

Final construction of the canal and bridge. The bridge was removed to facilitate Phase 2 road improvements in the 1990s.

The canal used to connect the harbour with Paradise Lake but now passes under the road into the Atlantis Marina.

shallow draught could then gain access to the pond. After extensive landscaping, the entire area was transformed into a scene of interest and beauty. As a final touch, Burnside's Pond was re-christened with the more glamorous name of Paradise Lake.

On Paradise Lake, near the harbour canal, Wenner-Gren constructed a boat house which also served as a guest house. He must have felt something like a Venetian doge when he received guests who came to his domain by that quaint waterway. Even this work, inspired by altruism and a taste for beauty, was thought by the rumour-mongers to have a sinister purpose. The canal to the north, they surmised, was designed as an entrance for German submarines. Through it they would enter Paradise Lake and there refuel and take on supplies of food and water. The fact that the depth of water in both the canal and the lake was far too shallow to accommodate a submarine was insufficient evidence to squash the rumour.

America entered the war on 7 December 1941, after the Japanese attack on Pearl Harbour. A month later a blacklist was issued naming more than a thousand firms whose activities were deemed to be pro-Axis or otherwise inimical to the Allied cause.[10] Wenner-Gren's name was on that list, a stigma which he thereafter always insisted to be undeserved and which he was successful in eradicating in 1946 after the end of the war.

Soon after the blacklisting, a group of Nassau-based soldiers and police carried out a thorough search of Shangri-La, but found nothing incriminating.[11] The *Southern Cross*, rumoured to be bristling with Beaufort guns, was also fruitlessly searched and the radio room sealed. Stories of the ship being armed survive to this day. John Dahllof, however, who was a member of the crew during the *Southern Cross*'s entire stay in Nassau, asserts that he never saw a weapon on board, other than a small pistol such as sea captains are accustomed to have at hand.[12]

Wenner-Gren, naturally, resented this harassment and left The Bahamas for a Mexican visit. He received a warm welcome from officials of that neutral country, especially when he let it be known that he was considering a $100 million investment in highways, railroads and industrial plants.[13] Although these grandiose ventures never materialised, Wenner-Gren's trips to Mexico became more frequent and more prolonged. He built a sumptuous residence and finally settled there for the duration of the war.

Throughout the war, however, and even afterwards, his agents continued to purchase plots of Hog Island property. At the end of hostilities, Wenner-Gren returned to Hog Island to spend the winters at Shangri-La as he had done before. But he could no longer undertake the glittering projects which had formerly excited his imagination. His finances were running low, some say because of indiscrete management by his underlings.

Early in 1961 he sold his Hog Island holdings to Huntington Hartford II for $9.5 million.[14] When negotiations for the sale of his Hog Island property were completed, he bought a Nassau home, Villa Capulet, and there he spent his last winter in The Bahamas.[15]

He returned to Sweden and continued to dream of paradises up to the time of his death in November 1961, at the age of 80. Some of his last thoughts were of a new and more elaborate Shangri-La which he hoped to build at Andros.[16] One can only hope that, somewhere beyond the skies, the old industrialist has found a perfect and eternal Shangri-La.

12
Huntington Hartford II

Geoffrey Johnstone, a prominent Nassau attorney, has always had a love for fishing. In the early afternoon of a Saturday in April 1959 he put aside his law books and concentrated his thoughts on the piscatorial pleasures which lay ahead of him. While in the process of closing his office door he was approached by a stranger who insisted that he needed some urgent legal advice and Johnstone, being an obliging man, consented to hear him out.

Huntington Hartford.

The stranger explained that he was a New York lawyer presently employed by Huntington Hartford, and that he was disturbed by an agreement which his boss had signed. So saying, he handed Johnstone a piece of paper which was, in fact, a menu from a private home named Shangri-La. On the back, in handwriting, it stated in the simplest of simple language that Axel Wenner-Gren agreed to sell, and Huntington Hartford to buy, Hog Island for $20 million. This curious document was signed by both men.

The New Yorker was not sure that he could dissuade Huntington Hartford from purchasing the property but he was convinced that the price was too high. What really agitated him was the thought that the 'agreement' might constitute a point of no return. And what he particularly wanted to know from Johnstone was whether the 'menu agreement' was a binding contract, under Bahamian law. Johnstone assured him to the contrary and he was much relieved. The result of this encounter was that Johnstone had to practically forget fishing for the next eight months because of his preoccupation with Hog Island and the enigmatic man who wanted to buy it.[1]

Huntington Hartford was born with the proverbial silver spoon in his mouth. Grandson of George Huntington Hartford, founder of the Great Atlantic and Pacific Tea Company (A & P), the fifth largest corporation in America, his inheritance was reported to be somewhere between 50 and 70 million dollars. During his early manhood he was content with the life of a playboy, forming associations with a number of glamorous Hollywood stars, and finally marrying a cigarette girl of Ciro's restaurant.

Then, at the age of 40, he seemed to have found his *raison d'être*. He burst on the world of art as a patron and critic. His severest censures were directed at the abstract-expressionist form of painting which became popular after World War II. As he saw it, painters and writers of the nineteenth century had achieved a perfection which was being trampled underfoot by the 'moderns'. His many writings on the subject were collected together in a book called *Armageddon of Art* – the final and conclusive battle between the forces of good and evil. He saw himself as a crusader on the side of 'good'.[2]

He was not to be a passive fighter, but one who was prepared to throw all his talents and fortune into the battle. He established the Huntington Hartford Foundation Art Colony on 154 acres in California with the object of guiding budding artists in the 'right' direction. Some who applied to enter the colony were turned down because they were 'too abstract'.[3]

Among his other expensive projects were: a million dollar legitimate theatre for Hollywood; a graphology (handwriting analysis) institute; a $862,000 gift to New York City for a Central Park café and pavilion, and a $7 million Gallery of Modern Art in the Columbus Circle, New York City. The latter, built of white marble and ten stories high, is the tallest art museum in the world.[4]

His sister, Mrs J F C Brice, had been a long-time winter resident of Nassau and it was probably through this connection that he first became acquainted with The Bahamas. Being a sailing enthusiast, he was soon captivated by the clear and beautiful sea. In 1959 he bought a house and two acres of land on Hog Island from the estate of Eleanor Harris, and in this home he installed a Chinese bed which was capable of marvellous gyrations. Those who saw the contraption were convinced that it served the purpose of a mechanical aphrodisiac.

Hartford soon got to know Wenner-Gren and the two undoubtedly conversed a great deal about Hog Island, its attributes and its future possibilities. The acquaintanceship of these men was probably looked upon by each of them as a fortuitous occurrence. By that time, Wenner-Gren was faced with a downward spiral of income, and he was seriously thinking of divesting himself of his Hog Island holdings. Hartford, flushed with money, saw the island as an opportunity to indulge his artistic ambitions and, in the process, to do something he had never done before – make money.

One night the two men dined together at Wenner-Gren's secluded home on Hog Island, Shangri-La, and during their convivial evening they impetuously drew up and signed the 'menu agreement'. As pointed out by Johnstone, this 'bush lawyer' agreement was not quite valid for a number of reasons, and Hartford's advisor thought the sale price far too high. But Wenner-Gren remained anxious to sell and Hartford to buy.

After protracted negotiations and the injection of legal expertise, Hartford finally agreed to buy the property for $13 million on 6 February 1960. Part of the purchase price ($7 million) was secured by a mortgage payable over a period of years. Wenner-Gren subsequently reduced the amount of the mortgage by $3.5 million as an inducement to earlier payment.[5]

The new owner's plans for the island differed in one very important respect from those of his predecessor. Whereas Wenner-Gren looked on his estate as his private Shangri-La to be enjoyed only by his wife, himself and their friends, Hartford was looking at the commercial possibilities. Here he was, comfortably established in his own house with the Chinese bed, looking about to see what could be made of Wenner-Gren's holdings, Shangri-La and the boat house; but before making his decision, he wanted a change in the name of the island. 'Hog' did not appeal to him. He was in agreement with Wenner-Gren, who is reported to have said that 'Hog is an ugly name – the island should be called Paradise'. These two men were convinced that Shakespeare's assurance about the rose smelling as sweet by any other name, could not apply to the name of Hog Island.

Hartford petitioned the Government to change the name and on 23 May 1962, by an Act of the legislature, it was decreed that: 'From and after the coming into force of this Act the Island lying to the North of the

Shangri-La and Ocean Club Restaurant.

Island of New Providence heretofore known as Hog Island shall be called and referred to as Paradise Island'.

Adjacent to Wenner-Gren's Shangri-La, a 52-room hotel and four double-bedroom cottages were built. This exclusive complex, planned for the accommodation of visitors and a centre of activities, was named the Ocean Club. The boat house was renovated and tastefully furnished in attractive French decor, and it reopened its doors as the Café Martinique. Hurricane Hole, after improvements, was made into a first class, 65-craft yacht basin. New changing-room facilities, a solarium and a restaurant and lounge were among the other developments at Paradise Beach. Near the eastern end of the harbour foreshore, reclamation and bulk-heading of an area known as Three Bays added 42 acres of land to the island. On this and adjacent land, an 18-hole golf course was constructed.[6] Then because his wife was fond of horses and equestrian sports, Hartford built a compound, called the Stables, to promote horsemanship.[7]

While all these works were in progress, many of which were carried on simultaneously, he spent a fortune on landscaping his property, exhibiting always a great deal of interest and knowledge in this field.

There were many small boats engaged in the ferry and sea-gardens business, in transporting workmen and materials across the harbour, and other activities associated with the island. To keep this fleet in good condition, Hartford decided to construct a small marine railway and shipyard.[8] There remained the problem, however, of getting visitors to the island in a pleasant way. The old method of having them come by the 'Sea Gardens and Paradise Beach' ferries was thought to be unsatisfactory. The bridge of Prince George Wharf, the place of embarkation, was an unattractive and untidy area and the ferries themselves, frequently referred to as 'Bum Boats' were lacking in smartness, safety, comfort and efficiency. All in all, it was a poor door through which to enter Paradise.

Hartford set out to improve this aspect of a visitor's experience. He purchased a $650,000, two-and-a-half acre site on the Nassau waterfront to be used as a terminal complex. The building erected there contained a lounge and a bar with an adjacent patio-restaurant called the Mermaid Tavern. The entire area was charmingly landscaped with beautiful tropical foliage. On the waterfront, sturdy docks were constructed to accommodate two imported ferries capable of carrying large quantities of goods and materials required for the improvements in progress on the island. In addition, a fleet of safe and comfortable ferry boats was acquired, and these, romantically named 'water taxis', whisked guests across the harbour of Nassau at frequent intervals according to a fixed schedule.[9]

At any function which took place on the island, Hartford was inevitably surrounded by a bevy of young and beautiful girls. This gained him the reputation of being a womaniser. Some people, with thoughts of the Chinese bed, even spoke of him as a Lothario. Those who came to know him well never doubted his ability to spend money recklessly, to attract members of the opposite sex or to cultivate beautiful surroundings, but as to his business acumen, they were not so sure.

Some time before Wenner-Gren sold his property, he had begun the creation of the Versailles Gardens with the object of embellishing the surroundings of his Shangri-La.[10] Here he endeavoured to create an atmosphere similar to that of the historic Versailles gardens of King Louis XIV of France. When Hartford took over he was, naturally, thrilled with both the idea and the work which his predecessor had initiated, and he continued to improve the gardens during his years of ownership. Thus this beauty spot can be looked upon as the handiwork of both men.

Stretching from Shangri-La (now the Ocean Club) to the hill slope near the harbour, the gardens extend for a quarter of a mile in a north–south direction. They are terraced into seven levels. As they ascend upwards, the various plateaux are accentuated by hand-laid rock ridges and stone steps. Focal points at each level are provided by pieces of original sculpture, many of

Versailles Gardens.

The Cloister.

which were carved from the beautiful white marble of Carrara, Italy.

Flanking the entrance are two statues of Josephine, wife of the Emperor Napoleon. She is depicted in a reclining position as if inviting visitors to contemplate the beauty stretching before their eyes.

Further up, in the centre of a lily pond, is a life-size statue of Hercules, carved in Greece probably in the late twelfth century. On each side of this classic masterpiece are two giant bronze statues, one of Franklin D Roosevelt and one of David Livingstone, the two men Hartford most admired.

Further on up the ascent again, is a small but beautiful bronze sculpture called 'Mother and Child'. It is interesting that this particular work, done by Dick Reid in 1920, was placed in a storeroom on the island some years before and forgotten. It was found by an employee who questioned Hartford about it. 'It is like finding a lost treasure', Hartford said.

Another memento to Wenner-Gren is situated near the crest of the gardens. This statue, once owned by the Swede, is of Gretchen, Mephistopheles and Faust. A twelfth-century pedestal is the base for a sundial, which was added in relatively recent years; the base is a typical piece of gothic art.

The gardens are indeed a scene of singular attraction and timeless beauty.

Across the roadway from the gardens and up a flight of stone steps stands an interesting structure on the very crest of the hill. This is The Cloister, an edifice of great interest to visitors. A fourteenth-century Augustinian cloister, this structure was purchased in France a number of years ago by the American newspaper magnate, William Randolph Hearst, who had it taken down and brought to Florida where the pieces remained in crates. The lot was subsequently purchased by Hartford who employed J J Castreman, an expert in the recreation of stone structures, to reassemble the cloister on Paradise Island.

To Castreman's astonishment there was not a single written clue as to how the stones were to be put together. Consequently, the reconstruction took a full year. It is a

The Cloister.

roofless structure with multi-columned sides and many arches which lend grace and beauty to the austere interior. In the centre of The Cloister stands a white marble statue of a meditating madonna. In its original time and place, the cloister had a fountain in the centre, around which monks walked while engaged in prayer.[11] We are unable to say how many people go there to pray or meditate today, but a large number of bridal parties look on The Cloister as a romantic background for the taking of wedding pictures.

Down the other side of the hill, looking across the harbour and on to Nassau is a small Greek gazebo which once stood in the garden of Shangri-La. Hartford had it moved to its present commanding position. It is called a love temple with rounded seats for those who like just to sit and think about the days gone by and the inscrutable future which lies ahead.[12]

Huntington Hartford and President Richard Nixon.

It is estimated that Hartford spent $10 million on improvements which, when added to the original purchase price of $9.5 million, constituted an enormous outlay, even for a man of his wealth. Furthermore, the income from his venture was distressingly small, while the cost of keeping it going was astronomical. Looking at it all in retrospect, it is easy enough to see that too much was spent on the gratification of personal whims and a love of embellishment and not enough on viable projects.

Hartford belatedly realised that he was getting into a predicament. On the one hand he wanted to hold on in the hope of reversing the downhill course, and on the other hand he knew he could not hold on much longer without exhausting his financial resources.

He looked about for some sort of magical inspiration that might inject new hope into an increasingly desperate situation. And his mind turned to Freeport, Grand Bahama. Paradise Island from 1964 to 1965 was in much the same situation as Freeport had been in 1962. It was not paying, and further development was grinding to a halt. Wallace Groves had looked about for some means of putting his floundering project on its feet, and he became convinced that casino gambling would do the trick. Groves had applied for a licence and it was granted on 1 April 1963. On the last day of that year, a large modern hotel, replete with a sparkling casino, opened its doors. And from that day Freeport took on new life and began an exciting march forward.

The example was there for Hartford to see, and the idea of a casino infused him with the hope he so badly needed. He approached Sir Stafford Sands, Minister of Finance and Tourism, and the man to see in matters of that magnitude. Sir Stafford offered no encouragement. What he said in effect was that he agreed in essence that Paradise needed a casino but that it could not be justified under the present ownership and degree of development. But should Mr Hartford care to sell a majority interest in his holdings something might be arranged.[13]

The facts are that at that particular time Sir Stafford had already engaged in talks with some clients who were anxious to buy Paradise and infuse a new fortune into development, provided they were granted a casino gaming licence. Sir Stafford had a confidence in this group that Hartford could not engender.

In desperation, Hartford tried one final tack in an effort to hold on to his beloved Paradise. On 15 November 1963, he decided to place the issue before the public. A statement released to the media called attention to the opening of a casino at Freeport and raised the question as to whether such an attraction should also be allowed in the Nassau area.[14] He stressed the benefits to be derived from casino gambling.

In talks with prospective investors, Hartford had become convinced that he could 'immediately put up at least one thousand, first-class hotel rooms and other facilities' costing $20 million or more – if gambling were permitted. His final pitch was an offer 'that 50 per cent of the entire net profit of a Paradise Island Casino would go to the Bahamian Government for the specific purpose of improved housing, medical care and social welfare'.

This was something like a last shot for Hartford; a shot which had no positive results. The rapid depletion of his wealth became a worrisome matter to Hartford, a man who had not been troubled with such serious financial problems before in his life. Reluctantly, he came to the conclusion that the only way out of the financial morass was to sell the island as suggested by Sir Stafford. Preliminary talks with the potential buyer, the Mary Carter Paint Company, indicated, however, that negotiations towards that end threatened to be complicated and protracted.

In the meantime the expenses at Paradise were continuing with not nearly enough income to meet them. Hartford approached Sir Roland Symonette, Premier of The Bahamas and laid the problem before him. Sir Roland responded by lending Hartford one of his most trusted and competent men, Roy MacKeen, with instructions to reverse the cash flow.

When MacKeen arrived at Paradise the owner immediately handed him a typed paragraph which he was requested to copy in his own handwriting. Among his accomplishments, Hartford considered himself to be talented in the esoteric art of handwriting analysis, and all of his key men were required to submit to that test.[15] MacKeen, having apparently passed the graphology test, was allowed to proceed with his efforts to correct the imbalance between expenditure and income. And the only practical way to do this was to close down those parts of the operation which were not viable.

The Ocean Club with its 52-room hotel should have been a money-maker, but it was overstaffed and a large number of its occupants were Hartford's friends who paid no money. It was closed. The Hurricane Hole Marina and Shipyard, both money losers, were leased to Symonette's shipyard. The Café Martinique, the Golf Club and Stables were also shut down. To say the least, there was little activity going on at Paradise after this severe pruning. Only Paradise Beach and its facilities remained as a throbbing remnant of a dying dream.

MacKeen offers some interesting insights into the causes of failure. At the top of the list he places Hartford himself – a talented man who had lived a protected life and who had never felt the necessity of learning the strictures of business.[16] Even while his empire was crumbling about him, he moved with a distracted air as if he were divorced from reality, his mind still absorbed with heady and profitless ventures. The second most obvious cause of failure was to be found among his echelons. Some of these men, thought to be competent after handwriting analysis, were completely useless in practice. However, they knew the boss's ways and soon discovered they could hold on to their jobs and even gain advancement by seeing that he was provided with the sort of pleasures he enjoyed.

When the sale finally came through in January 1966, Hartford retained a 25 per cent interest and for a few years he continued to take an active part in company affairs. His job was chiefly that of an advisor in matters of beautification. But, even without the drain of Paradise, he was not able to alter his lifestyle sufficiently so as to live within his means. Always needing more money, Hartford was compelled to sell his quarter-interest in Paradise and all his other Bahamian holdings. The sale of his private home was inclusive of 'goods and chattels' which Hartford discovered, to his chagrin, included his Chinese bed.[17] This was, perhaps, the unkindest cut of all!

13
Resorts International

*R*esorts International has a short but interesting background. In 1958 the attention of
John Crosby, a retired Washington Attorney and former Assistant United States
Attorney-General under Woodrow Wilson, became attracted to the old Mary Carter
Paint Company as a business investment. Co-partners in the acquisition were Governor
Thomas E Dewey, Lowell Thomas and a number of other distinguished persons.

A year later, James M Crosby (son of John), who was then President of the Unexcelled Chemical Corporation, was named Chairman of the company. I G Davis, Junior, became President and a director of the Paint Company the following year. Under the guidance of these two men the company experienced increasing success as a manufacturer and distributor of paint and related products.

James M Crosby.   *I G Davis Jr.*

The slogan 'Buy one gallon; get one free', was frequently heard by Bahamians over the Florida radio stations. Eventually Mary Carter Paint became available in The Bahamas through the Kelly's Hardware outlet, although the free gallon did not manage to cross the Gulf Stream with the rest of the paint.

Soon after they gained control, Crosby and Davis set about diversifying the company's activities. In 1962 the National Biff Burger System was acquired. This chain of restaurants was primarily engaged in the selling of low-cost foods through fast-service, roadside outlets. After

adding this subsidiary to its business portfolio, the Paint Company took on an international aspect by purchasing Bahamas Developers Ltd., a Freeport, Grand Bahama company engaged in developing and selling land at Queen's Cove.

Freeport did not show much promise at the time of the purchase – but there were plans afoot which augured well for its future prospects. A gaming licence had been approved by the Government in April 1963 and on the last day of that year the luxurious Lucayan Beach Hotel, replete with an attractive-looking casino, opened its doors.[1] This development proved to be the long sought catalyst of success and Freeport began to move. The Paint Company had invested at a propitious time and within a few years it sold millions of dollars worth of home sites.

Encouraged by their first Bahamian venture, Crosby and Davis then turned their attention to Paradise Island which was up for sale. The island had not been a financial success and its owner was stymied in his efforts to make it a viable development. Crosby and Davis, in consultations with their legal advisor, Sir Stafford Sands, prepared proposals which were accepted by the Government and which were designed to put the island on its feet. The first stage of development included a 500-room hotel, a gaming casino, a theatre and a bridge linking the island to Nassau.[2]

The casino threatened to present a problem and it was left to Sir Stafford to overcome the obstacles. Sir Stafford was more than a brilliant lawyer; he was the Minister of Finance and Tourism in the Government of the day and the man to see when legislative approval was needed with respect to any sizeable tourist enterprise. When he had engineered a casino for Freeport, Sir Stafford had been compelled to use all the ingenuity, and even deviousness, he could muster. But Paradise Island was a different 'kettle of fish', for whereas Freeport was looked upon as a distant outpost, Paradise was on the doorstep of the capital. If a casino was proposed for that island, the protests could be expected to be more vociferous than those raised against the Freeport casino.

The Minister's fertile mind conceived of a plan to make the casino more palatable to those who were opposed to organised gambling. The old Bahamian Club on West Bay Street had possessed a gaming licence for many years. This pre-war establishment operated only during the winter season and was something of an anachronism when seen in the light of post-war, year-round tourism and the booming casino at Freeport. In Sir Stafford's eyes it was a waste of a gaming licence. Willard McKenzie and Frank Dineen, owners of the Bahamian Club, were persuaded to surrender their licence with the object of it being transferred to Paradise. Agreement to this arrangement passed through the legislature with relative ease.

The Mary Carter Paint Company acquired a majority (75 per cent) interest in Hartford's holdings in January 1966 and immediately infused new energy and capital into Paradise.

But less than three months after the Paint Company had entered the scene, the eastern section of the Ocean Club was burnt to the ground.[3] This had been Wenner-Gren's tastefully decorated Shangri-La which Hartford had converted into a high-class tourist facility, the Ocean Club. From Nassau the billowing smoke and flames made quite a show on the northern skyline. Two fire fighting units, with portable equipment, were sent by boat from Nassau, but all efforts to extinguish the blaze were futile. Apart from the building, the loss of the kitchen equipment, valuable furnishings, paintings, silverware and liquors represented an enormous sum. A business consultant for the Paint Company estimated the total loss to be in excess of a million pounds.

There was a comical side to this catastrophe. The fire attracted hundreds of workmen to the site. These men discovered the wine cellar before the fire had reached it, and they reasoned that it was preferable to drink the contents rather than leave them to feed the flames. As a result, something akin to a drunken orgy formed the periphery of the devouring flames.

The next day Crosby and Davis let it be known that the loss would in no way affect their development plans. In fact, at the time of the fire, construction plans were already progressing at a vigorous speed.

Ferries had served their time well in the cross-harbour transportation of the public. From rowing boats and sailboats through primitive steam launches to Hartford's modern water-taxis they had done a splendid job. And, no doubt, those who took the ferries looked on the ride as something of an adventure.

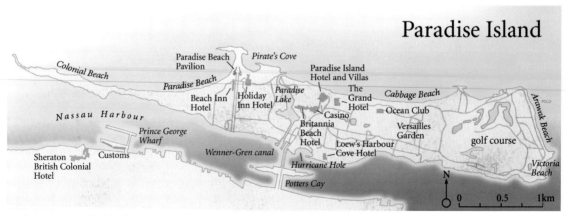

Developments on Paradise Island up to 1983.

Centre of Paradise Island with bridge.

Cabbage Beach), soon resounded with the excited voices of arriving and departing guests.

The casino, joined to the hotel by a short, covered walkway, sprang to life as if by magic, with a fairyland atmosphere of glitter and glamour. Gazing on the scene was like peering into a kaleidoscope of brilliant colours and ceaseless motion. The half-acre gaming field hummed with a peculiar sound of its own, a blend of hundreds of conversations interspersed with peals of laughter, the rustling of elegant gowns, the clinking of ice-cubes, the clicking and clattering of dice and chips, and the distinctive sounds of more than 300 whirring slot-machines.

By 1966, however, a flood of tourists approaching the one million mark was arriving annually at Nassau's International Airport. If Paradise were to succeed it was necessary to attract a good percentage of these visitors, and the ferry system, however quaint, was seen as a bottleneck.

The bridge, 1,500 feet long, with a 70-foot high clearance for boats, was completed in March 1967, and by the end of that year a deluxe 500-room hotel with an adjacent casino and theatre was opened to guests. Paradise was ready to move. Comfortable and modern in every respect, the Paradise Island Hotel, situated on the one-and-a-half-mile long Hartford Beach (formerly

Paradise Island's casino.

Resorts International Paradise Island Resort.

Holiday Inn, Paradise Island.

The Flagler Inn became the Loew's Harbour Cove Inn and is now the Holiday Inn Sunspree.

Construction of the Grand Hotel.

The Grand Hotel, Paradise Island.

Le Cabaret Theatre, just off the casino, with a Radio City size stage, presenting a dinner show with a 650-person seating capacity, soon established its position as the premier theatre of The Bahamas. Employing elaborate production numbers and top entertainers, Le Cabaret offered an unexcelled experience in dining, dancing and theatre enjoyment.

Two years after starting out at Paradise, it became evident to the proprietors that their island subsidiary would overtake the parent paint company in growth potential and investment returns. Consequently, in May 1968 the net assets, business and name of the Mary Carter Paint Division were sold and the company changed its name to Resorts International, Inc.

Paradise at that time presented a rapidly changing scene as construction took on the aspect of a building boom. Two additional hotels were built in 1969: the 270-room Britannia Beach (now Atlantis Coral Towers) near the Paradise Island Hotel (now Atlantis Beach Towers), and the 250-room Flagler Inn on the harbour side. The Flagler (now Holiday Inn Sunspree) was at a disadvantage in not having a natural beach frontage. To overcome this, an inlet was scalloped out of the solid rock, and with nature's co-operation and approval a small, but fine, sandy beach soon appeared and was given the name of Shipwreck Beach.

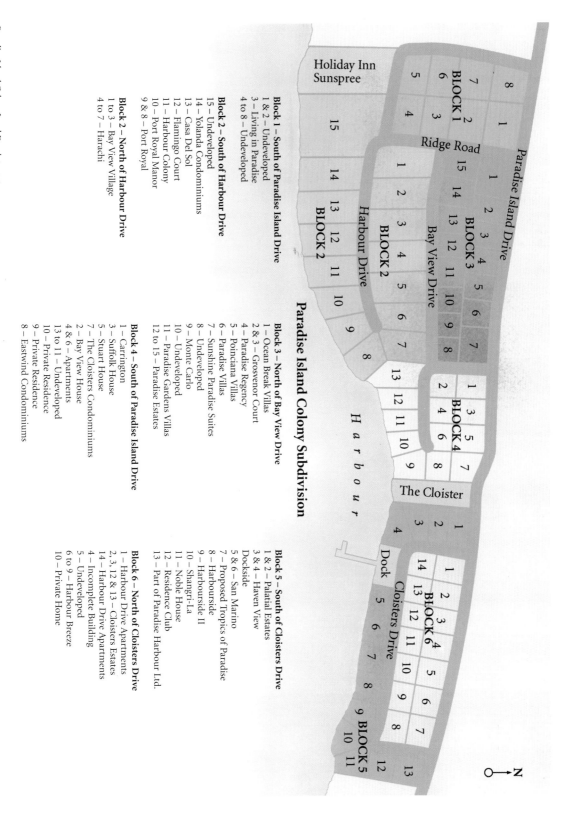

Dining at the Ocean Club.

units in the main building, cabanas and villas, it boasted nine impeccably maintained Har-Tru tennis courts, which have attracted some of the world's top professional and amateur players. Other developments sprang up on or near Cabbage Beach, namely the Sunshine Beach Club and Villas, Villas in Paradise, Miramar Beach Club and Villas and Paradise Island Beach Club. On the world-famous Paradise Beach was located the 100-room Beach Inn of traditional Bahamian architecture. Its beach pavilion, which offered magnificent vistas of sand and sea, was a favourite spot for dining and the enjoyment of light entertainment.

Not all of the hotels on Paradise were owned by Resorts International or operated by them. The company had shown remarkable flexibility in the utilisation of its valuable property and in attracting capital. It sold land to prospective builders of hotels, condominiums and private homes. The buildings on the land between the harbour and Paradise Island Drive mushroomed from the early 1970s when John Eaton, an American, built Grosvenor Court. Then in the 1980s, Cavalier Construction Company and others built and developed Paradise Island Colony Subdivision and in no time condominiums, villas and apartments, for rent and privately owned, dominated the harbour side.

Between Paradise Beach and Hartford (Cabbage) Beach there is a secluded bay called Pirate's Cove. This picturesque location was chosen as the site of the Holiday Inn (533 rooms). Completed in 1971, this structure had the distinction of being the tallest hotel in The Bahamas. In 1982 an addition of 350 rooms was made to the Britannia Beach, which more than doubled its accommodation. And in that same year the Grand Hotel (350 rooms) opened its doors. Other facilities, smaller but worthy of mention, included the elegant Ocean Club Hotel and Tennis Resort. Containing 71

A tract of about 30 acres which Resorts claimed was disputed by a private group, and the Courts decided in favour of the adverse claimants. But apart from this tract, Resorts International owned all the land on Hog Island except the western end and certain lots which

Seaplane landing at Paradise Island.

Florida and Paradise. Using amphibious aircraft, several roundtrips were made each day, and passengers found the low altitude flights to be convenient as well as different and exciting.

When Crosby and Davis first came to Paradise, perhaps thinking of Hartford's failures, they announced that it was not their intention to develop a millionaires' retreat. Rather they planned a tastefully done resort area with an appeal to both the very wealthy and the general Nassau tourists. It was to be different from anything The Bahamas had to offer. It wasn't the wilderness of Andros, nor was it another Miami Beach.[4] In looking back to those days one can only conclude that these two businessmen must have had a clear-sighted vision of the road to success. And they trod that road with unswerving persistence. These men did not make headlines outside of business matters. Whatever whims and eccentricities they might have had, they did not come to the public's attention. Crosby and Davis were in the class of 'hard-headed American businessmen'.

Although Resorts International branched out into other areas, Paradise remained the hub and showpiece of its enterprises. Also, it was a significant contributor to the company's earnings.

they had sold to others. The company's total holdings were approximately 600 acres.

With all the hotels trying to get their share of the tourist dollar, the competition was keen in a subdued way, each one trying to gain some superiority through its own specific attractions. On the other hand, the degree of co-operation among them all was striking. They introduced what was called 'Goombay Madness', a programme of entertainment in which all Resorts International's hotels and locations took part and to which all guests on the island were invited. It included a roast suckling-pig feast, a high tea and fashion show, a junkanoo jamboree, a backgammon tournament, a local song and dance revue, climaxed by a Goombay festival, featuring native food and entertainment.

The interchange programme permitted guests at any of the company's hotels to charge dinner, drinks, entertainment and recreation expenses to their own hotel-room account. The result of this policy was that guests could virtually look on the whole of Paradise as their vacation land and use all the facilities and attractions available.

The 18-hole golf course at the eastern end had a fully stocked pro-shop. The course, set out in beautiful surroundings, summoned every ounce of the player's skills, and called for the use of every club in the golf bag.

An unusual addition to the company's assets was made in 1974 when it bought Chalk's International Airline, thereby establishing a direct link between

Water sports.

Resorts' path to success was not entirely smooth. In 1972 it became known that Resorts and Robert Vesco were engaged in talks related to the sale of Paradise Island, including the casino complex.[5] The asking price was said to be between $65 million and $80 million. Although Vesco was not then the pariah he was later to be, the American Securities and Exchange Commission was having a close look at him and his handling of some mutual funds involving many millions of dollars. Vesco was a frightened man and anxious to establish a base outside the orbit of American jurisprudence. Perhaps the Government frowned on the sale and especially on the transfer of the casino licence. But whatever the reason, nothing ever materialised from these discussions.

Cabbage Beach.

Water skiing.

It seems that Hartford soon became discontented as a minority shareholder. His attitude was exacerbated by his impecunious circumstances. Claiming that Resorts and others were engaged in a conspiracy to take advantage of his 'illiquid position to wipe out his stockholding in Paradise Island', he took the issue to the American Courts in 1973.[6] After more than a year of litigation, the matter was resolved by private agreement. In exchange for certain financial considerations, Hartford agreed to stop his legal action and convey his Paradise shares to Resorts.[7]

Resorts admitted, in 1976, that during the previous five years it had made substantial contributions to Bahamian political persons and parties.[8] There was nothing illegal about this and since neither the donor nor the recipients were prepared to divulge any particulars, the potential political storm was not generated.

This and other similar incidents, which came along to ruffle the feathers of Resorts, had no adverse effect on the progress of Paradise Island. More important, by far, was a policy statement by Finance Minister, Arthur D Hanna, relative to casinos. In November 1973 he announced to Parliament that beginning in January 1978, all casinos in The Bahamas would be wholly owned and controlled by the Government.[9]

That had to be a worrisome matter to those who controlled Resorts, for the casino was by far the most remunerative of all the company's operations on the island. However, after three and a half years of anxious negotiations, an agreement was arrived at with the Government whereby the company was granted a managerial contract to run the Paradise casino for ten years. The terms of the contract were not made public and we can only assume that they were deemed to be satisfactory to both parties.

Resorts International wrought an amazing transformation of Paradise Island. All the construction that took place was accompanied by beautiful landscaping which, in many respects, enhanced the freshness, cleanness and charm, which first attracted visitors there so long ago.

But of great importance to the Bahamian people was the island's contribution to the economy. Undoubtedly it came as a surprise to many to read a news story (November 1981) which stated that Paradise Island had surpassed New Providence as a tourist centre.[10] As evidence of this, the article cited more hotel rooms, more workers with higher pay and more construction investment. Paradise was also shown to be ahead in 'many categories of revenue resources including rooms, food and beverage sales'. The writer, basing his

Couple at a pool bar.

Paradise Village shopping centre.

conclusions on Government statistics, ended by saying: 'And so the phenomenon, which has been the perceived reality for years, has finally been documented and that is Paradise Island and not Nassau is the mainstay of this country's tourism business'.

In the early 1980s Resorts International was looked upon as a good and valued corporate citizen. It had accomplished much on Paradise Island and prospered and many hundreds of Bahamians owed their livelihoods to the success of this progressive company. Wenner-Gren made an accurate observation when he said: 'Labour has never benefited for any length of time under a setup by which capital cannot also benefit'.[11]

For most of its history, Paradise (Hog) Island had been looked upon largely as the backyard of Nassau – a repository for things thought to be too dangerous or, for other reasons, not wanted in the capital. Resorts International changed all that and the island became very much the front porch of the capital with a very positive role to play in the large tourist and leisure industry.

14
Donald Trump

*I*n the late afternoon of the 19 May 1983, pandemonium broke out as a crowd of 50 angry guests gathered round the front desk of the Britannia Beach Hotel and threatened to punch the manager and sue the hotel.[1] They found that even though they had reservations, there was 'no room at the inn' as the hotel had overbooked. A few weeks before this incident, 6,000 tourists had to be 'put up' in private homes because of overbooking in Nassau and on Paradise Island.

The slogan, 'Its better in The Bahamas' coined by the Ministry of Tourism in its latest $16 million advertising campaign, had been too successful. While the Minister of Tourism, Perry Christie, could say, 'tourism is healthy', the satisfied but not complacent hoteliers recognised that more hotel rooms were necessary. Full occupancy over the winter season and record topping figures in June with a successful Goombay Madness brought an increase of 40 per cent more tourists. The struggling Eastern Airlines recognised the opportunity for profit and increased their seating capacity on flights to Nassau by 44 per cent. During the

next winter season the Paradise Island hotels were again flooded with visitors.

Encouraged by the growth, George R Myers, President of Resorts International Bahamas, announced, in January 1984, the Paradise Island Resort and Casino Consolidation, joining together the Paradise and Britannia Towers to become the world's largest complete resort and the largest private employer in The Bahamas. The complex now offered 1,147 luxurious guest rooms and a 20,000-square-foot casino. Tibor Rudas produced a new show called 'Dazzling Deception' at the Le Cabaret Theatre. The show was deemed

Cabaret dancers.

elaborate and costly; each lead dancer wore $5,000 worth of feathers and body jewellery to the value of $4,000. Further, Resorts agreed to purchase the recently liquidated Paradise Beach Inn and by October 1984 it re-opened as a 100-room 'sporting activity hotel' under the name 'Paradise Bahamas Getaway'.

At the same time, the Paradise Island Tourism Development Association was formed to create an alliance between the Paradise Island Hotels and the Nassau/Paradise Island Promotion Board, and to work closely with the Ministry of Tourism. The Association aimed to maintain high standards and offer a variety of activities between The Grand Hotel, Holiday Inn, Loew's Harbour Cove, Ocean Club, Paradise Beach Inn, Paradise Island Resort and Casino as well as Chalk's Airline. It is interesting to note that also joining the Association was Club Land'Or, overlooking Paradise Lagoon, the first luxury time-sharing complex, built in 1982.

Underneath these waves of success, a deep counter current flowed. Although, over 2 million visitors per year came to The Bahamas, the amount of money they spent in The Bahamas was relatively small. The many cruise ship passengers stayed only a few hours and numerous stopover visitors were on package deals. 'T shirts at 3 for $10' and 'Made in Taiwan' replaced 'English quality goods' as Bay Street began to take on a dirty, seedy look, where drugs could be obtained easily. One visitor wrote to the Editor of *The Tribune* that because Nassau was so dirty he was glad he stayed on Paradise Island, despite the expensive restaurants. Another tourist staying at the Paradise Island Resort and Casino complained that the recently instituted, compulsory 15 per cent gratuity, an incentive to provide high quality service, had backfired, and in fact a rude, lazy, uncaring attitude was the order of the day.

Despite the growing adverse publicity in the world press, Resorts decided to pump $11 million to expand the Casino by 50 per cent, build the 100-room Reef Club at Coral Towers and generally upgrade facilities. They also embarked on an aggressive marketing campaign. It seemed like a dog chasing its tail. World headlines, 'A nation for sale' drew attention to the escalating drug trade and the involvement of Bahamian officials. A year-long commission of enquiry determined that

drugs were creating social and economic problems and attracting the wrong kind of visitors.

The oil crisis, created by the 1984 Iraqi blockade of the Iranian Oil Terminal, placed additional financial burdens on an already unprofitable airline route to The Bahamas. Nassau International Airport was deemed too busy, inefficient and lacking in security against the growth of international terrorism. Passengers became annoyed at the many problems encountered and by 1985 tourism was said to be in a tailspin after continued negative publicity abroad. Paradise Island, despite full occupancy in the winter seasons, also suffered, as a long lasting worldwide recession adversely affected the tourism industry.

In April 1986, James M Crosby, Chairman of Resorts International Inc., died following respiratory surgery. I G 'Jack' Davis, President, announced that Resorts International Inc. would continue to remain under the control of the Crosby family and that Crosby, with his foresight, had made provision for the day-to-day operations and long-term objectives. He had laid out a blueprint and it would continue to be followed. We are not privy to the plans laid out in the blueprint but one aspect seems to stand out as foundation of the overall success of the company and the carrot for subsequent take-over bids.

When Resorts International was born in 1968, Crosby had the vision of owning and operating casinos around the world. Preparing for the advent of gaming in Atlantic City, Resorts bought property and Resorts International Casino Hotel became the first gaming resort to open in Atlantic City. Competition from other newly built casinos compelled Resorts to start the Taj Mahal Casino project but they were unable to complete it due to financial difficulties. The death of Crosby caused speculation on the American Stock Exchange that Resorts could become a takeover target.

At this time, Manhattan real estate mogul, Donald Trump, was prowling the Atlantic Boardwalk. In 1984, Trump became a partner in a joint venture with Harrah's Hotel and Casino at Trump Plaza and soon acquired the Atlantic City Hilton, renaming it Trump Castle. In March 1987, Trump, with one eye fixed on the Taj Mahal, decided to buy a 'pivotal chunk' of Resorts International from the Crosby family, which gave him

Resorts Casino in Atlantic City.

67 per cent of the voting power. A group headed by New York Attorney, Frances Purcell, offered more and the matter had to be decided by a Florida Probate Judge, who decided, in accordance with the Crosby family's wish, to accept Trump's $79 million offer, as they trusted him to complete the Taj Mahal.

Donald John Trump, born in New York in 1946, inherited his father's skill of recognising a good business deal and used it to support his family after his father's early death. After graduating in Finance from the University of Pennsylvania, he moved from Queens to Manhattan, concentrating on making business contacts at exclusive clubs. In 1987, he boasted, 'nobody's ever done what I have done at 41'. At that time he was running four casinos, five hotels and two skating rinks. While living in a penthouse atop Trump Towers, Trump spent weekends at his 50-bedroom, 30-bathroom mansion with a nine-hole golf course at Mar-de-Largo, Greenwich, Connecticut. His ultimate joy on the sea was

Jack Davis, Donald Trump and George Myers reveal plans for Paradise Island.

a 286-foot yacht with a disco, helipad and 45 telephones, on land a stretch limousine and in the air a helicopter and a 727 jet with two bedrooms and a sauna. His flamboyant lifestyle said to be as opulent as an oil sheik's, and his beautiful escorts made him a popular figure in the tabloids but led to his divorces from first wife Ivana and then Marla Maples.

Perhaps guided by Crosby's blueprint, Trump had big plans for Paradise Island. In November 1987, he revealed that Resorts would spend $57 million on the expansion of Paradise Island including a new luxury 150-room tower and water features, a redesigned Ocean Club, an upgraded golf course and a new 3,000-foot airstrip. In reality little of his plan was realised during his fleeting ownership. The golf course was upgraded and a few improvements made to the infrastructure of Paradise Island. It is perhaps ironic that Trump prided himself on his architectural ability and his soaring ambition was to build the world's largest building yet he built nothing on Paradise Island.

Huntington Hartford had conceived the idea of building an airstrip but rejected it because aircraft would only be able to take off and land in one direction.

To bypass the busy Nassau International Airport and traffic congestion, Crosby had proposed a jetport on Athol Island with a bridge over to Paradise Island. Howls of protest came from citizens, championed by Lynn Holowesko, President of The Bahamas National Trust, who felt that such a project would be detrimental to the environment. Trump was already experienced in short distance air travel as he owned a fleet of de Haviland Dash-7, 48-seat planes shuttling gamblers from Philadelphia to Atlantic City. In September 1987, despite protests from the Chamber of Commerce and political opponents, the land at the eastern end of Paradise Island was cleared to build an airport.

By the time the airport was completed, Trump was no longer the major shareholder of Resorts. That honour fell to his arch rival, Merv Griffin.

15
Merv Griffin

In the lighter days after World War II novelty songs were popular in bars and on bus trips as easy sing-a-longs, much as karaoke is enjoyed communally today. A favourite, one of the top songs of 1950, was I've got a lovely bunch of coconuts *sung by a young $125 per week band singer called Merv Griffin. This rising celebrity starred on radio and in the movies, and then moved to television, first as a singer, then as an easygoing talk show host and on to his own profitable game shows* Wheel of Fortune *and* Jeopardy. *In 1986, Merv Griffin Enterprises were sold to Coca-Cola for $250 million as Merv bought into hotels because in his own words, 'After years of living in hotels I cultivated a passion for the hospitality business'.*

Merv Griffin.

'Bring people in, entertain them and give them a reason to come back' was his motto. His hotels became choice venues for the annual Golden Globe awards and other high profile events. Behind the easygoing geniality, Merv had quite a practical side: 'the three primary needs for

the traveller are quick check-in, fast room service and excellent water pressure'. With this philosophy, Merv was successful at the Beverly Hilton Hotel, where he insisted that guests were given a warm welcome and caring personal attention. He believed that superb facilities and amenities in a spectacular location would make the guest want to visit again. Merv quickly added hotels in California, Arizona and Ireland to his portfolio as he observed the marketplace and provided what was lacking.

Merv bought Resorts International because he believed it could become a valuable company but he did not take over without a fight. In March of 1988, two of America's richest men, the affable Merv Griffin and the brash Donald Trump squared off in a battle for control of Resorts International. Trump held most of the voting power but Griffin offered more money and when the dust settled after months of lawsuits and counter lawsuits, Griffin came out ahead, saying 'Closing the deal with Trump was like World War III'. The total price tag was said to be $300 million, but the company was $600 million in debt. Griffin acknowledged that Trump was a wonderful contender and they remained business partners in Atlantic City, where Trump retained control of the Taj Mahal. Later, at the opening ceremony of the Taj Mahal, Griffin, as Master of Ceremonies, respectfully introduced Donald Trump to the audience.

Enthusiastic as ever, Merv announced that although there would be no new drastic policy or managerial changes, the Griffin Company would bring new ideas and restore Paradise Island to its former greatness. These promises came at a time when The Bahamas was experiencing very poor winter seasons in tourism. A drastic decline in air visitors, competition from cruise ships, troubled relationships with trade unions, poor image of The Bahamas abroad and a recession in the American economy all contributed to the decline in the tourist industry. The conditions at Paradise Island were so bad that 1,200 workers were working a four-day week. In general, Merv took over at the time when Paradise Island was considered as overpriced, and tourists were flocking to Mexico and other destinations.

In June 1988, Merv came to Paradise Island for the first time to meet Prime Minister Pindling and the Bahamian people. In November the new owner, full of fun, spirit and enthusiasm, hosted a 20-minute segment of the Le Cabaret show, introducing himself and his executive board to the Paradise Island employees and news media, and stressing that employees were an important part of the team. From that day T-shirts proclaiming 'I am on Merv's team' became the standard uniform. He outlined his plans for Resorts International, which included renovation of the Paradise Towers and the need for extensive landscaping.

High on the agenda was a promotion of Bahamian culture, emphasising that he didn't come to The Bahamas to hear Stardust but rather Bahama Mama.

True to his word, he constructed an attractive roundabout complete with native flowers and a cascading waterfall situated such that it was the visitors' first sight as they left the bridge and entered Paradise. The roadways and green areas took on an aesthetic and natural look, as Merv spent $2 million to convert the drive from the bridge into a lush tropical setting. To build team spirit, he held an Employees Appreciation Day to salute the 3,400 employees. And Merv captured international media attention by highly publicised visits of celebrities such as Zsa Zsa and Eva Gabor and Vanna White, who loved to slip over the bridge for 'crack conch' at Potter's Cay.

Vincent Vanderpool Wallace, George Myers and Merv Griffin announce plans for Paradise Island.

Paradise Island Airport.

On the 10 April 1989, the first turquoise and yellow de Haviland Dash-7, with passengers from the USA, touched down on the tarmac of the brand new Paradise Island Airport, welcomed by the calypso beat of the Police Band. An excited and thrilled Merv Griffin, Sir Lynden and Lady Pindling and 300 guests witnessed the opening of the new facility, which incorporated the existing Chalk's Seaplanes and the new Paradise Island Airlines. The daily capacity rose from 175 to 475 passengers to and from Miami and Fort Lauderdale and later West Palm Beach and Orlando, allowing people from around the world to filter to Paradise Island and at the same time becoming a convenient air transport route for locals to travel to the USA on flights as frequent as 14 per day.

While Merv strove to make Paradise Island beautiful, clean and friendly, and tried to ensure guests were satisfied and entertained, other factors worked against him. Cabbage Beach, used for picnics by local people, playing loud music, was often left dirty. Jet skis became dangerous to swimmers as they were often driven recklessly and their owners sometimes harassed the relaxing visitor. The Paradise Island Condominium owners were unhappy about the noise of the blast of the turbo prop engines taking off from the airport. However, these were relatively minor problems compared to the financial difficulties of Resorts International.

By August 1989, Merv announced that Resorts was short of cash, as operational cash flows were less than

anticipated and it had taken the company longer than expected to sell non-operating real estate. By April 1990, Paradise Island Resort and Casino was up for sale after an aggregate net loss of $302 million, and they filed a voluntary petition for bankruptcy in order to reorganise the company. And the following December the financially troubled Resorts sold off Chalk's Airline to United Capital Corporation, Illinois, for an undisclosed sum. To add to the woes, Clement Maynard, Minister of Tourism expressed his grave concern about The Bahamas' image as a tourist destination. Hotels faced a grim winter season and the occupancy at Resorts was dismal. Similarly, the Sheraton Grand Hotel and Holiday Inn were forced to cut back on staff, close restaurants and reduce salaries temporarily, until the hotels could reach a profitable level.

Paradise Island Airlines' plane.

Despite the difficulties faced at some of the larger properties, optimism prevailed elsewhere on Paradise Island. In 1986, Club Land'Or completed a three-quarter of a million dollar renovation programme. A group of developers from Virginia had introduced The Bahamas to this first time-sharing luxury complex in 1982, which allowed foreigners to buy an apartment for one week of the year for a period of 20 years. Situated on the south-eastern edge of the Paradise Lagoon, Club Land'Or aimed to blend southern style Virginia hospitality with the warm smile and friendliness of the 30-member Bahamian staff. The guests were kept occupied by a variety of fun filled activities, which included barbeques at Rose Island, a Bahamian band, limbo shows and live piano music by John Clarke in the Oasis Lounge. The close-knit family atmosphere of the complex and the shared facilities of the casino and golf course, under an agreement with Resorts, proved to be successful and profitable.

In August of 1990, the Marriott Hotel Group signed a joint venture with Cavalier Construction Company to manage and market the existing Paradise Beach Club, another time-sharing complex, located on the north shore of Paradise Island. Under this agreement another 130 two-bedroom units were to be built on the 7-acre site that included 700 feet of beachfront overlooking Cabbage Beach. The complex, already a favourite with international visitors, became even more popular. The partnership lasted until January 2003, when Hans-Peter Kugler and Partners took over the Paradise Beach Club.

In 1991 Kugler and Partners had shown the clearest indication of confidence in building Paradise Harbour Club and Marina, a time-share resort and health spa. Situated on the harbourside, towards the eastern end of the island, the club caters to affluent world travellers wishing to relax either in one of the 23 luxurious apartments or at the 28-slip marina. The guests can dine at the Columbus Tavern or by the natural beauty of the rock garden waterfall overlooking the harbour.

About the same time, Comfort Suites was constructed by High Point Development Company and opened on 21 September 1991. The hotel had 'ready made' pre-fabricated rooms, which helped keep the cost and building time to a minimum. A group of local businessmen, headed by President Leroy Bowe, agreed to build the 150-room hotel in a 'land for shares swap' to help Resorts International fulfil its obligation to build 250 rooms in exchange for permission to enlarge the casino. Resorts had added the 100-room Reef Club at Coral Towers in 1986 but financial constraints prevented adding the further 150 rooms to their property. Within a year, Comfort Suites was awarded the International Hotel of the Year by Choice Hotels International and the following year, the Gold Hospitality Award for attention to hospitality and guest satisfaction.

In December 1990, the 250-room Loew's Harbour Cove transferred ownership to Four Stars Resorts headed by Iranian, Joseph Moinan. The new owner was really excited and promised to make a lot of changes, but did little other than the name change to Harbour Cove Inn. In May 2000, the 246-room hotel was taken over by Driftwood Ventures and renamed the Holiday Inn Sunspree.

The Gulf War of January 1991 caused over 3,000 travellers to cancel bookings and airlines were only flying at 50 per cent of full capacity. In the first quarter of 1992, Resort's earnings dropped dramatically from $2.5 million to $1.25 million. Throughout 1991 and 1992 the continued decline in the tour and travel industry due to recession in the USA and fierce competition from Cancun, Barbados, Virgin Islands and Hawaii, all offering attractive discount rates, challenged The Bahamas' position as the number one tourist destination in the Caribbean. Hotels were becoming expensive to run and inflation was eating into their earnings as the increased competition decreased room rates. Perhaps the worst indictment of all was the inherited design defects of the 1960 box style of concrete and glass buildings, like the Holiday Inn, that were incongruous with the spectacular location of Paradise Island.

At the end of August 1992, the Free National Movement led by Hubert Ingraham delivered a landslide victory in the General Election, ousting Pindling's Progressive Liberal Party. Just as Ingraham declared Government in the sunshine, Hurricane Andrew devastated The Bahamas. Paradise Island was about to take on 'a new lease on life'.

16
Sol Kerzner

By early 1993 it was recognised that the falling hotel occupancy was more due to changing trends in the region's tourism industry than to worldwide economic recession. Competition from other destinations was a factor, but the rise in popularity of cruise ships, with many companies sponsoring three or four-day cruises, also contributed to the diving occupancy rates in the New Providence and Paradise hotels. Additionally, when in port a cruise ship visitor spent an average of $70, in contrast to an average of $840 for the hotel visitor. It seemed obvious that a new approach was necessary if the New Providence and Paradise Island hotels were to survive.

The wind of change was in the air. A prominent tourism expert in Nassau, Conrad Zeilman, warned that casinos, glitter and glamour did not attract Europeans. The Bahamas should broaden its advertising strategy to highlight other aspects, especially the natural beauty of the islands. People were looking for travel experiences to enrich their lives, and to enhance their personal growth and quality of life. The newly emerging tourist market was no longer found inside the walls of casinos but in the expressions of local culture and in the roots of historical heritage.[1] The new Government immediately announced that ecotourism would become a powerful instrument for development, and introduced the new slogan, 'It's hip to hop to The Bahamas'.

The new approach was to be spearheaded by an unlikely candidate, a South African by the name of Sol Kerzner, who at the time was seeking to expand his South African hospitality business and enter the marketplace in the United States of America. Sol first came to The Bahamas in the early 1970s as a young man in the hotel business. He had heard about Paradise Island and wanted to see the development there. He was literally there for 24 hours but time enough to be awestruck by the exquisite beauty of the beaches and the ocean. He was captivated by the breathtaking sight of the bold Atlantic waves rolling onto the pristine, powdery sand and knew that there was no other such place on Earth.

As a young boy, Sol, born in 1935 to Russian immigrants in a poor Johannesburg suburb, helped sell everything from chips to chewing gum in his family's café. While qualifying as a chartered accountant, Sol became the South African University's boxing champion and the wrestling champion of the University of Witwatersand. His disciplined approach and business acumen were obvious early on as Sol worked in an accounting company and assisted his parents in running a small hotel in Durban. Soon after, he leased the Palace Hotel, and then bought the Astra, which he sold at a profit. His first big gamble was his investment in an underdeveloped site on a stretch of beachfront at Umhlanga Rocks, a tiny fishing village near Durban. With backing from his former accounting clients, Sol built the first South African five-star hotel, the Beverly Hills Hotel, which featured the new concept of a complete resort, combining a variety of sports and entertainment facilities with a good mix of specialty restaurants and bars. One year later in 1965, the hotel was acclaimed a premier resort for local and international tourists. In the following years, Sol proved beyond any shadow of doubt, that as far as first-class hotel development was concerned, he had the Midas touch. Success followed success as he built the 450-room Elangeni, and along with South African Breweries, established a chain of 30 Southern Sun luxury hotels. The South African Institute of Marketing Management awarded Sol the Marketing Award of the Year in 1978 and 1980.

Sol sold his shares in Southern Sun in 1983 to focus on Sun International (South Africa) and concentrate on casino resorts both for Southern Sun and Rennies Consolidated Holdings. In 1992, he completed the $267 million African-fantasy theme resort, The Lost City at Sun City, the most ambitious resort development in South Africa, featuring a 62-acre man-made jungle and the Valley of Waves, a giant pool big enough to hold surfing competitions. With local success behind him, Sol was now ready to turn his attention to international development. By a magical coincidence he was approached by Lazards, a group of investment bankers, to see whether his company was interested in acquiring the bankrupt Paradise Island Resorts.

Sol flew over to see if the beaches and ocean were as he recalled. He immediately recognised the potential as he again saw the incredible coral sand beach and the warm translucent waters' shifting hues from the deep blue of the Atlantic Ocean to the opaque greens of the seashore. The warm ocean breezes swept over the island an aura of mystique and serenity that was compelling. The exciting prospect of transforming 200 acres of undeveloped land offset the run down condition of the Resort International properties and King Midas could not resist the challenge.

Jackson Burnside, a prominent local architect, was hired to survey and produce digital drawings of the whole resort. His team, manning five computer stations, took over the Andros Room of the Britannia Beach and working 24/7, produced the required disks in short order. After due consideration, Sol thought that previous owners had failed because they did not make a big enough investment, but he was willing to take a risk, despite the misgivings of his Directors. Since the property was in the hands of bondholders, the negotiations took a long time, but were finally concluded on 3 May 1994.

The consolidated Paradise Resorts, now known as Atlantis, were placed in a new company named Sun International Hotels Limited. To breathe life into the run down properties, the first phase of Sol's proposed

Sol Kerzner with his worry beads.

transformation required extensive rebuilding and renovation at an estimated cost in excess of $100 million. And time was short since the winter tourist season was only seven months away. Local banks were sceptical but Scotiabank believed in the potential of the project and agreed to a significant loan.

One thousand men were put to work ripping everything apart, and every restaurant, every lobby, and every kitchen was rebuilt along with extensive remodelling, revamping and upgrading of rooms. Miraculously, on 22 December 1994, the 1,147-room Atlantis opened with a greatly enhanced waterscape containing water attractions, swimming pools, numerous lagoons, a living saltwater habitat, and an open air marine habitat housing over 100 species of marine life in millions of gallons of water. Entertainment featured a world-class casino, fine themed dining, golf, tennis and water sports. The following month, the newly rebuilt Ocean Club opened its doors in its well-established tradition, as an exclusive, high-end resort. Phase 1 was complete at a cost of $140 million.

Howard 'Butch' Kerzner, Sol's 35-year-old son, joined the venture as President of Sun International. At the time he was described as a young, aggressive, focused, self-motivated businessman but admitted that in the early days after the opening of Phase 1 he looked at the previous day's takings with trepidation. Because they desperately needed cash flow they had to open the hotel even as construction was still taking place and one big winner in the casino could have really hurt financially.

The aim of the company in Sol's words was 'to blow away the customer'. The result certainly blew *Tribune* columnist, Nicki Kelly away as she wrote:

Butch Kerzner.

Atlantis is everything The Bahamas must have been before civilisation took hold – a tropical fantasy land. There is a feeling of ethereal tranquillity that buoys you as you drift through this tropical Shangri-La. The physical features dictate the design. The flood of natural light has transformed the physical features of the ugly, dark Britannia Beach. The spectacular native gardens – all native vegetation – are an integral part of the interior design. The furnishings are rich but understated; every facet is an expression of good taste; attention to detail in the decoration gives the sensation of being pampered on a wealthy landowner's estate. The sense of intimacy has been achieved by seemingly endless numbers of special areas for a variety of activities; there may be thousands of people but one is only aware of a few at a time. The winding pathways lead to one pleasant surprise after another from caves to waterfalls to lagoons and to any number of charming restaurants; there is no loud music, instead muted piped music blending with the running water.[2]

A spirit of excitement and confidence pervaded the whole country. Investors were impressed and encouraged by the investment incentives of the new FNM Government, and Sol Kerzner provided the leadership for sound hotel development not present for some time. It was felt that the Atlantis creation would become the hottest destination in the region and create a mushroom effect touching every aspect of the Bahamian community. The former Paradise Island Resorts had experienced a five-year decline to 60 per cent occupancy even with very low room rates; Atlantis turned this around and in the first year the occupancy rate rose to 85 per cent and the room rates increased by 30 per cent. In that short time Atlantis became a tourist magnet and its success, plus the amenities it had to offer, inspired other business ventures on Paradise Island, Nassau and The Bahamas in general.

In April 1992, the Sheraton Grand celebrated its tenth anniversary with a multi-million dollar refurbishing programme but sustained damage during Hurricane Andrew, and after another $1.5 million was spent, the hotel switched affiliation to the Carlton Hospitality Group and became known as the Radisson Grand Resort. By 1995, the Holiday Inn had undergone image alteration, placing emphasis on family vacations. The Harbour Cove Inn, benefiting from a steady stream of investors, became the Paradise Island Fun Club. On the mainland, Breezes purchased the Ambassador Beach Hotel, Sandals bought the Royal Bahamian Hotel and the new owners of the British Colonial Hilton announced a $100 million restoration of the historical landmark opposite the entrance to the harbour. The Bahamas, with modernised tourist facilities, was set to become the premier destination in the region.

Sun International made an effort to target the upscale family market in the United States with a multiple marketing strategy, using unprecedented two-minute commercials, which offered attractions to the whole family including the casino, restaurants, outdoor activities, great scuba diving and especially Camp Paradise for children. They attracted media coverage of special events, hosting the World Lightweight Boxing Championship, The World's Strongest Man, The Atlantis Super Boat Challenge and International Golf and Tennis Classics. Marketing in Asia was also successful; by the end of 1996 the number of Asian tourists had doubled to 18,670 from the total given in 1990. The largest contingent was from Japan but others came from Hong Kong, Philippines, Taiwan, Malaysia, Indonesia and Singapore. About four per cent of Sun's business came from Japan and it was noted that they liked to shop; in fact one Japanese tourist paid $700 to have her hair braided!

Hoteliers in The Bahamas were thankful as tourists filled their rooms for the 1995–1996 winter season. Atlantis was bursting at the seams having sold all 1,147 rooms. The spin off for the Bahamian economy was amazing. Sun International's presence had resulted in the use of many Bahamian professional services in agriculture, fisheries, decoration and most of all jobs. It was projected that 30 additional jets would fly into Nassau every month, resulting in increased revenue for taxis, straw-workers and shopkeepers. The Government was set to benefit from increased real property tax, electricity, telephone, water and other services.

In his many years in the hotel industry, Sol recognised the value of staff training, not only in the skills needed to complete their job, but also in the attitudes and behaviour towards the guests, who expected friendliness and good treatment, in a top class establishment. Sol brought groups from London and Dallas to provide training for local employees to develop their people skills. Within a few months the feedback showed a high level of satisfaction among tourists, who were pleasantly surprised at the warm hospitality of the hotel employees. Sun International instituted award ceremonies for employees, who excelled in the services provided.

The Minister of Tourism, Frank Watson, praised Atlantis as a milestone for tourism in The Bahamas, saying that the success of the first phase exceeded all expectations by transforming the image of Paradise Island and Nassau. In addition to greater employment, the completion of Phase 1 brought a substantial increase in foreign exchange, greater opportunity for Bahamian businesses and an expanded market for arts and crafts. Most of all, The Bahamas had been accelerated onto the world stage as a tourist destination, and the Atlantis resort was the largest outside Las Vegas.[3]

But the competition was not standing still. Disney, the pioneer of theme parks to entertain the whole family, opened the huge Animal Kingdom and instigated a twice weekly Disney Magic cruise ship with 2,000 passengers per visit to Castaway Cay, Abaco. Multi-million dollar theme hotels became the order of the day as Las Vegas realised that gaming alone did not drive the hotel business. In quick succession, The Bellagio with an Italian theme and botanical gardens, The Luxor with an Egyptian theme and The Excalibur with a medieval theme opened to accommodate the change in travel trends, where family fun became much more important. A poll of Atlantis guests revealed that only 20 per cent of guests chose Atlantis for its casino, but 92 per cent gambled, many just playing the slot machines.

Although by September 1996 The Bahamas was the top tourist spot in the Caribbean, there was the critical issue of 'airlift'. There were more hotel rooms available than airline seats to fill them. Despite efforts by Government, airlines were leaving The Bahamas for more profitable routes, and Kerzner was worried because prospective guests and conventions were booking rooms, but cancelling because they were unable to fly to The Bahamas. To assist the situation, Paradise Airlines offered three daily services to Orlando, as many tourists liked to spend a week at Disney World and a week in The Bahamas. Fortunately, by November 1998, there was a 25 per cent increase in airline seats as daily services were started by TWA and Delta from New York, Commair from Cincinatti and six daily flights from Fort

Lauderdale by American Eagle. British Airways added another flight from London and several charters began from London and Paris. Chalk's Airline made yet another revival and resumed flights to and from Miami, Fort Lauderdale and Bimini.

But Sol was ahead of the game. When he first took over, he realised that he had to do something really unique on Paradise Island to be able to compete into the next century. In his mind he had already captured African fantasy, Mohegan Indian heritage and legend and was also thinking about the mystique of the desert in Dubai. We can only speculate on how many sets of his gold worry beads he wore out, as he rebuilt and completed the waterscape of Phase 1 and ruminated about Phase 2 of Atlantis.

To understand how Sol's imagination works we have to understand how he thinks and what he believes in. To say he is a busy man is an understatement. Sol spends 80 per cent of his time involved in new projects and development, travelling the world but spending long periods at a site when he needs to create and guide the construction. He admits things get hectic but he never sacrifices quality time with his whole family. In the summer, they spend three or four weeks at his villa in the South of France or his house in Oxford, England, and for Christmas and New Year the family gather at their luxury estate close to Cape Town, South Africa. Sol uses his leisure as leisure should be used. He concentrates his attention on the people he loves and the many family activities that take up every parent's time. And no one knows better than the man responsible for providing holiday experiences for millions of people, the value of a vacation. During the time relaxing from the pressures of working life, the mind somehow acts like a coffee percolator, and those scattered random thoughts like magic form into a new grand idea.

As Phase 2 took shape, Sol, team captain of the multi-talented design team, which included the architects of Wimberly, Allison, Tong and Goo, spent 18 months researching the myth of Atlantis and the lost Royal City slowly emerging from the sea. As usual, Sol

was 'hands on', involved in every detail, every discussion, every concept of the whole design. The architecture and atmosphere was to be inspired by sea life and the decision made that although a new casino would be built, the resort would be family oriented.

Phase 2 was a pretty bold project that would benefit the Bahamian economy, especially labour employment. One thousand two hundred construction workers were already employed but 10,000 man-hours would be worked by the end of Phase 2. And Sun's total construction investment over four years would be $800 million, including $50 million spent on local purchases. Almost immediately, Sun announced plans for a $17.5 million Marina at Atlantis as Sol sought Government support to promote and develop The Bahamas as an overall tourist destination to compete, not with other hotels in the country, but with other destinations like Orlando, Mexico or Las Vegas. In December 1997, Sun International, in conjunction with Vistana Inc. of Orlando, Florida, announced plans to build time-share

villas on the harbourside, with hopes of attracting a very upscale market.

During this productive period of construction, local residents were shaking their heads as road crews, telephone, water and electrical workers tore up the infrastructure of New Providence and Paradise Island.

The whole country seemed noisy and dusty, and travelling anywhere was a challenge. But by the end of May 1998, after many years of rumour, speculation and months of preparation and planning, the roads of New Providence were repaired and the traffic flow reversed. Similarly, the roads, utility access and conduits on the 826-acre Paradise Island were completed with eight-foot wide sidewalks and street lights every 70 feet. To alleviate the lack of parking space for staff and guests, Sun International built a three-tier parking lot for 1,200 cars at a cost of $15 million.

For Bahamians, the last few months of 1998 were perhaps the most memorable in the century. As talk of Year 2000 was heating up, forecasting disaster for computer related businesses, Paradise Island witnessed some momentous changes.

Construction workers on Atlantis had been housed at the 27-year-old Holiday Inn, which held two records. When built, it was the highest building in The Bahamas, and for one day, the highest building ever imploded, a process which took 418 pounds of explosives and 20 seconds to complete.

By a strange quirk of fate the hotel on West Bay Street, formerly called the Atlantis, re-opened as a new Holiday Inn.

In early October, the spectacular 50,000 square foot Atlantis Casino, the first in the world to be suspended over water, opened, and guests witnessed first hand the fantasy design features, the multi-million dollar chandeliers, the marble floors and sea-view marine habitats. One cocktail waitress said she had been trained for the previous seven weeks in anticipation of the opening. Baha'men, a leading local band, entertained the visitors, who revelled in the gamblers' delight of 1,000 slots and 80 gaming tables. The Five Twins gourmet restaurant provided hand-rolled cigars and rare wines, and Dragons Discotheque, late night dancing.

On 12 December, a fanfare by the Police Band and fireworks marked the opening of the $20 million second Paradise Island Bridge, which took 14 months to build.

Implosion of the Holiday Inn.

Aerial shot of the two bridges.

The three-lane bridge, owned by the Government and financed by Government bonds and a toll, was expected to generate revenue of $10,000 per day. Two months later repairs began on the old bridge, and long suffering Bahamians and Paradise employees could look forward to trouble free motoring, going to Paradise over the new bridge and returning to Nassau on the old.

The biggest celebration of all came with the opening of the 23-storey Royal Towers on the 14 December when Sol's most ingenious dream had become a reality. From the time the giant cranes capable of 300-foot lifts arrived on site, it was a very challenging and tight two-year schedule to do things that had never been done before. New, innovative technology was needed to build the biggest marine habitat in the world. Sol loved working with Dale Chihuly in Seattle on the Temple of the Sun, but the glass blower was astounded when Sol asked him to blow glass twice the size he had ever blown before. The Mayan Temple, with the first slide shooting through a shark tank in acrylic tubes, presented great engineering difficulties, but Sol and the builders were very excited with the idea and rose to the occasion. Tired, but with a twinkle in his eyes, Sol recalled the

years of planning, the sleepless nights twirling his gold worry beads, the travelling, the negotiating and supervising endless streams of local and foreign workmen, all made worthwhile with that rush of adrenaline, that pride everyone feels, when the race is won.

As far back as April he had instigated the Sun Star Talent Search to find talented, passionate and committed Bahamians for employment opportunities in the massive expansion of Atlantis. Long lines of thousands sought a Sun job and all applicants took a ten-minute aptitude test to obtain an interview and were whittled down to 6,000 workers by December. All received specialty training, particularly the 40 graduates from Atlantis First Culinary Training Programme that gave in-house training for Bahamians in Atlantis' first class restaurants. Sol was determined to provide first class cuisine and service to his guests. With nervous anticipation the galaxy of players, including on centre stage one man with the worry beads, waited.

At last the big night came. It was a night to remember as 2,000 guests witnessed a very proud Sol Kerzner and Dolores, wife of Prime Minister Hubert Ingraham, cut a ribbon of seaweed and seashells symbolising the launch of the Royal Towers at Atlantis. This, along with the openings of the Animal Kingdom and the Bellagio, were the three most significant tourist events of the year and maybe the millennium. In the history of The Bahamas, the party was the largest, most lavish, most extravagant ever thrown, and was attended by some of the hottest movie, television and music stars. Among the most famous celebrities were Oprah Winfrey, Julia Roberts, Denzel Washington, Leonardo de Caprio, Donald Trump, Alfred Woodard, Sean 'Puff Daddy' Combs and Sir Sidney Poitier, alongside local political, religious and social dignitaries and hundreds of media representatives.

The guests were royally served by the newly trained staff with a variety of fine food and wines and entertained by a 300-strong Bahamian choir and by international artists: Bebe Winans, Stephanie Mills, Debbie Winans, Natalie Cole, Stevie Wonder, Ashford and Simpson, Patti Austin, James Ingraham, Quincy Jones and Michael Jackson. Everyone in Nassau witnessed the most astounding fireworks display that lit up the night sky making it seem as bright as day. Guests were awestruck as fireworks by Grucci cascaded from every balcony, to symbolise the rising of Atlantis from the ocean floor.

Like his hero Winston Churchill on VE day, witnessing the victory celebrations was a dream come true for Sol. All the sleepless nights, all the decisions and all the dedicated hard work had paid off. His goal was not just to build and operate a successful resort, but also to create a place as original from the outside as from the inside, and moreover one that was recession proof. Along with the Harbourside Resort, the Marina at Atlantis and the Ocean Club, Sol has created a complete and multi-dimensional complex, where guests are transported into a dazzling, imaginative world, where every sight, taste and experience immerses the visitor in the mysterious universe of Atlantis.

Fireworks at the opening of the Royal Towers.

Paradise Island

Lighthouse

Nassau Harbour

Prince George
Wharf

Atlantis
Marina

Harbourside
Vacation Ownership Villas

Ocean Club

Clubhouse

Ocean Club
Golf Course

N

0   0.5   1km

Paradise Island showing Kerzner International Properties and the lighthouse.

17
Atlantis

*O*nce upon a time the Gods were taking over by lot the whole of the Earth according to its regions. Poseidon took for his allotment an island which he called Atlantis after Atlas, the eldest of his five pairs of twin sons, who also gave his name to the Atlantic Ocean. The Greek philosopher, Plato, passed on the story told to the poet Solon by Egyptian priests, who said that the island was located in front of the 'Pillars of Hercules' (the Straits of Gibraltar), at the edge of the known world. Atlantis, governed by the laws of Poseidon, became highly civilised like Utopia, but as a result of portentous earthquakes and floods, the Island of Atlantis was swallowed up by the sea and vanished.

From the middle of the nineteenth century, scholars have tried to pin down the location of Atlantis, especially as it was predicted to rise again out of the Atlantic Ocean. A strong candidate, on the edge of the Great Bahama Bank, was Bimini, believed by Ponce de Leon to be the site of the 'fountain of youth'. The theory was that the flat undersea rocks along the Bimini shores were stones from the city of Atlantis. Another popular myth surfaced in the 1970s when it was rumoured that the lost city of Atlantis was located under the Yoga Retreat at Paradise Island.

It is a custom in The Bahamas that men of importance are invited to tea at Government House to meet the Governor and leading dignitaries. Over such a tea, Lady Darling, the Governor's wife, on hearing Sol Kerzner's enthusiasm about bringing the ocean and sea life into the resort, told him about the Bimini theory. Eureka! Sol loved the idea of Atlantis and his fertile mind ran wild. 'What I love about Atlantis,' he mused, 'it's a myth and has so many different stories, you can use your imagination. Atlantis can be located anywhere in the Atlantic Ocean from Europe to Mexico and the mystery gives a lot of scope to do fun things'.[1]

On the edge of the Great Bahama Bank and close to the Tongue of the Ocean, Paradise Island lies in a sheltered corner of the North-east Providence Channel. Its position protects it from the hurricanes that whistle

Sculpture of Atlas in the Atlas Grille and Bar.

up the Florida Straits to the west, or the windward shores to the east. And at the same time it enjoys the renewal and refreshment of the Atlantic Ocean at a point where the North-east Trade Winds are usually transformed into prevailing gentle east or south-east breezes.

For Bahamians and tourists alike, a day at the beach and a swim in the sea is one of life's simpler pleasures. The buoyancy of seawater makes us feel weightless and its coolness is refreshing. Even the sight of the sea is therapeutic. Sometimes beneath the clear water we notice the shadow of a fish, hanging motionless or flashing through the shallows in the ever-changing rays of sunlight, while the gulls circle overhead. The sight catches us right below the heart with a sentimental fascination and delight. We also enjoy the fright or flight sensation at the sight of the jumping barracuda or big sharks and manta rays as they glide effortlessly in search of their prey.

All this and the serene or violent beauty of the sea, sand and sky, Sol has captured with his concept of Atlantis, bringing us back from our isolation from nature. Like the city of King Atlas of old, Atlantis is virtually surrounded by water with the crystal clear ocean on one side, a 7-acre saltwater lagoon and the spectacular 34-acre waterscape, giving the impression of a royal city rising out of the sea.

Sol realised that most people want their lives to be more exciting and they are attracted to the extraordinary and magical. They are drawn to places of myth and legends that make them feel fully alive. Although Sol admits to some artistic licence, it is remarkable how close the Atlantis project is to Plato's story.[2]

The dramatic Phase 1 transformation of the Beach and Coral Towers and the 3.4 million gallon waterscape to the eastern edge of Paradise Lagoon suggested a re-emergence of a paradise lost, a modern garden of Hesperides. And the Phase 2 expansion to the west created an 11 million gallon waterscape, the sacred grove of Poseidon, with 'springs of abundant volume… sweet scented stuffs from roots, herbs or trees for food, orchards of fruit as well as remedies for sufferers; all

Water sports.

Atlantis surrounded by water.

these that island produced as it lay then beneath the sun, produced in marvellous beauty and endless abundance…They constructed many temples for gods, many gardens, many exercising grounds'.

An amble through the sacred grove of Poseidon reveals magnificent settings overlooking cascading fountains, shimmering lagoons and of course the glistening white waves and rolling surf of the Atlantic Ocean breaking onto the white, powdery sand of Cabbage Beach. The walkways meander between exotic native plants, under hidden grottos and caves and over bridges. The popular rope bridge, suspended over foaming waters, especially delights those who seek the thrill of the wild. The lush tropical foliage and the lagoons teeming with different species of local fish enhance the natural beauty of the grove. The lagoon is ever busy with water sport enthusiasts canoeing, paddle boating and fish spotting; the ocean as busy with visitors

The rope bridge.

swimming, snorkelling, skiing, banana boating, jet-skiing and parasailing. The life size replica of the ancient Mayan Temple is spectacular, and from its top, slides tempt the daring to high-speed rides through a shark filled marine habitat.

Mayan Temple.

A shark swimming in the Mayan Temple Lagoon.

Lagoon Bar.

Ceiling of the Lagoon Bar.

Among the many reminders of the Atlantean World is the fossilised ceiling of the Lagoon Bar, which gives the appearance of having been submerged for centuries.

Across the Paradise Lagoon and beyond the Royal Baths Pool, the Royal Walk leads to the north entrance of the Royal Towers with the eye-catching monument of Cypselurus. This 50-foot high, bronze and steel sculpture of 28 flying fish is the creation of Kathy Spalding, using a very old lost wax process. It is a spectacular lifelike resemblance of the Cypselurus, flying, gliding and diving into a fountain among jets of water. The flying fish Cypselurus spawn only in the Sargasso Sea, and the monument sets the mood for the artistic wonders of the lost city of Atlantis found inside the Royal Towers.

Monument of Cypselurus.

View from bridge of Royal Towers and Harbourside Villas.

Statue of flying chariot horses.

Plato tells us that the seaway and harbour were filled with many ships and that 'they bridged over the circles of sea which surrounded the ancient metropolis, making therefore a road to the Royal Palace, which they made into an abode amazing to behold for the magnitude and beauty of its workmanship'. As visitors travel over the new bridge to Paradise Island, they see 'framed of one simple colour', salmon pink, the Royal Towers rising majestically out of the sea and 'other buildings weaved in many colours so as to confer on them a natural charm'.

The Royal Road to the palace passes through the first Bahamian underwater tunnel beneath the entrance to the Atlantis Marina. As one approaches the Royal Towers there is an exquisite fountain with golden statues of Poseidon's six winged chariot horses.

The sculptor, Danie de Jager, actually used the frozen corpse of a horse to obtain the exact measurements of the statues. Plato's mermaids on the backs of dolphins have been replaced on the top of the hotel towers by Blue Marlins, the Bahamian national fish, which act as lightning conductors.

'They made an entrance to it from the sea and they roofed over it so that the sea became subterranean.' Alighting from the taxi, one is struck by the height and opulence of the spacious Royal Towers *porte cochere*, a shaded, cool, welcoming area abounding with the sights and sounds of the surrounding water.

Blue Marlins.

The two halves of the ancient looking bronze door, leading into the main lobby in the Great Hall of Waters, are engraved symbolically to ward off the dangers faced by the Atlanteans. Portrayed are a winged seahorse for protection from the air, a frightening fish-eel creature as a guard against sea attack and armed warriors against a land siege. Edging the door and encircling the seahorse, astral charms, to ward off evil, form an ornate frieze. To withstand the ravages of a force-five hurricane, a strong fibreglass material has been used in its design.

On entering the Great Hall of Waters, guests, like the Atlanteans of old, are overawed with the seven-storey high, ornate columns supporting a gold domed roof with a raised shell design.

The door to the Great Hall of Waters.

Great Hall of Waters.

Murals on the walls of the Great Hall of Waters.

The floor is magnificently tiled with marble of differing hues of pink and grey, interspaced with geometric and astral mosaics. The walls are decorated with eight colourful murals that depict the Atlantean life and beliefs. Sol, always seeking perfection, made three trips to Italy to choose marble for the Royal Towers, and Albino Gonzalez, a Spanish artist who did not speak a word of English, painted the murals.

After check-in the guests are shown up to their king or queen room or their suite, whether it be Regal, Grand, Presidential, Royal or the Bridge Suite. After settling in comfortably, it is very difficult to choose whether to experience Atlantean life inside the Royal 'Palace' or outside in the expanded waterscape.

Sol and his designers chose some of the best artists in the world to portray the mystery of the provocative legends of ancient Atlantis. The colourful map on the ceiling of the Pegasus Race & Sports Book depicts Atlantis as the omphalos, the navel of the world, surrounded by all other lands with their wonders: Stonehenge, Mount Olympus, Valhalla, Easter Island, Machu Picchu, Tower of Babel, Xanadu and Eldorado.

Ceiling of the Pegasus Race & Sports Book.

The murals on the walls depict adventurous voyages to these lands for discovery or trade. The bounty of these voyages can be found in the décor and buffet of The Marketplace, the mecca of the dining experience at Atlantis. Illuminated manuscript pages of Plato's story of Atlantis decorate the walls of Plato's Lounge.

Plato's manuscript Critias.

Picturesque wrought iron railings, made in Sheffield, England, divide the lobby from the Café of the Great Hall of Waters, situated down a marble staircase, alongside which, great black marble balls revolve in the swishing, gushing fountains of water, symbolic of the water flowing out of the rising Atlantis. The world's largest marine habitat surrounds the Café, allowing diners to marvel at sharks, grouper and all species of local sea-life as they swim among the ruins of Atlantis.

The Great Hall of Waters is spectacular but Sol had envisioned the greater splendour of one whole wall of glass fronting a marine habitat with whale sharks. Unfortunately the constraints of $480 million held him back just as much as we might be restrained with $48 thousand; the size of tank and amount of tuna to sustain the whale sharks were just too great a cost.

Darwin's theory of evolution drove archaeologists and anthropologists to Palestine, Greece, Egypt and many other exotic lands of the Middle East, where many

Local sea life in the marine habitat.

The Navigation Room at The Dig.

fantastic myths and legends originated. Charlie White III, founder of OLIO, specialising in imaginative entertainment environments, worked closely with the Atlantis design team to produce The Dig, a simulated archaeological site. This maze of underwater corridors and passageways among the ancient ruins of Atlantis is the home of exotic sea creatures, swimming amongst the toppled temples and statues, which are engraved with art and hieroglyphics explaining Atlantean culture and trade.

The highlight of The Dig is the Navigation Room, where the Atlanteans forecast the weather and planned their journeys by land, sea or air.

While discovering Atlantis can be classed as edutainment for the whole family, there is plenty of entertainment, excitement and relaxation offered at the resort. The 100,000-square-foot Entertainment Centre

Sea creatures swimming among ruins.

features the largest casino in the Caribbean, incorporating several themed restaurants and lounges. Dance floors swing to the music of live local bands and shows feature world renowned entertainers. In the casino, underneath the Chihuly crystal chandelier depicting sea life, high rollers can play baccarat at $10,000 per hand. More modest investments can be

made at any of the 78 gaming tables or the 980 slot machines, situated around the central Temple of the Sun with its fiery red and orange tentacles, and the Temple of the Moon, shaped by icy blue and white discs. These glass blown sculptures, along with the Crystal Gate, at one entrance to the casino, were also created by Dale Chihuly, while the Golden Bullfish at the Poseidon Throne entrance, were the work of Danie de Jager. The Atlas Sports Bar, The Five Twins and the statues and artwork in and around the casino are all designed to enhance the Atlantean ambience.

Seaform chandelier.

Temple of the Moon.

Temple of the Sun.

Crystal Gate (opposite page).

Golden Bullfish.

Poseidon's Throne.

From dawn to dusk guests have the use of the Sports Centre at Atlantis, featuring ten all-weather tennis courts and state of the art facilities for basketball, volleyball and swimming. The complex also houses a Fitness Centre and the $2.5 million, 11,500-square-foot Mandara Spa for massage and therapy of the body and soul. Golfers can play the 7159-yard, par 72 Ocean Club Golf Course, designed by Tom Weiskopf, to challenge their precision and accuracy, while enjoying the panoramic scenery and ocean breezes.

Luxury yachts up to 220 feet long can pass through the 100-foot wide entrance to the new spacious, five-star Marina at Atlantis with 63 slips. Facilities equalling those at Monte Carlo are available and sailors can enjoy all the amenities of the Atlantis Resort. Also sharing these amenities are the owners of the adjacent vibrant green, blue and yellow vacation ownership villas of the Harbourside Resort. These villas are a 50/50 partnership between Sun (Kerzner) International and Starwood Vacation Ownership Inc. providing the vacation owner with opportunities to vacation at any of Starwood's many properties around the world.

Reception lobby at the Ocean Club.

View of the beach from the Ocean Club.

One of Axel Wenner-Gren's ambitions was to build the world's largest aquarium near his peaceful Shangri-La, with its breathtaking view of the white sand and crystal clear waters. Like the winner of the last hand, Sol Kerzner has taken all and taken it to another level. The newly redesigned Ocean Club celebrated its opening in February 2002 with a new terrace of 50 elegant bedrooms, a new gourmet dining experience at the old Courtyard Terrace and the new chic beachfront restaurant, Dune. Created by Jean-Georges Vongerichten, a chef of international repute, Dune offers elegant dining in a British colonial atmosphere, the design of Christian Liaigre. A very attractive addition to the elite resort is the Ocean Club Spa, which opened in May 2002, and combines Asian rituals and holistic therapies with Bahamian herbal essences.

To achieve two other ambitions, Sol closed down the Paradise Island Airport in September 1999, as its limited facilities were not enough to service the increased flow of visitors, and levelled the existing golf course. He wanted to build a spectacular world-class golf course and to develop an exclusive gated residential community. The Ocean Club Estates, with residential lots overlooking the golf course and the ocean or harbour, sold out within a month for between a half million and three million dollars each. Michael Jordan, Barry Bonds and Ernie Els, the first Ocean Club golf professional, were among the early buyers. A new marina has been cut into the north-east of the development on the harbourside.

At the end of the second millennium, it was seen that several influential factors had shaped tourism. In the

East end of Paradise Island with the Tom Weiskopf designed Ocean Club Golf Course surrounded by the developing Ocean Club Estates.

United States, 'baby boomers' could expect a higher life expectancy and a shorter working week. The American economy was booming so many had greater leisure time and more money to spend. At the same time The Bahamas had kept apace with tourism trends, merging lodging with entertainment, and as a result hotels had full occupancy, the economy was booming and confidence was at an all time high. Sol Kerzner had led the revolution to offer a mix of the natural environment, themed attractions, activities and gaming to a clientele who appreciated health, learning and spiritual pursuits in an increasingly complex world.

Although many Bahamians enjoyed a reasonable standard of living from their success in the business community, there was room for improvement in certain social and educational areas. A big company like Sun International, with a 6,000-person workforce, realised that it must become like a godfather to the community. The economic boom consumed the talent pool faster than the educational institutions could replenish it. Therefore, training and community development became a priority for the company.

'Greatness lies in the detail' was the motto given by the Gentleman Butler Company, England, in training butlers, whose job begins before the guest arrives as they collect and co-ordinate everything in preparation. Recognising that the strength of a workforce is in its ability to pass on skills, Sun International engaged Langevin Learning Services to train the training personnel. Motivational seminars were held to enhance the idea that the customer is most important and the core value, 'blow the customer away', became the staff mantra. Staff were sent to London, South Africa, Asia, Las Vegas, Orlando, Sardinia, to other Sun International properties and locally for additional training in their area of expertise. After 9/11, a very special extensive training for the Atlantis security staff took place in December 2002. The Atlantis University was formed to promote management and leadership skills with the motto, 'Teamwork is the key to survival'. Sun International has recognised annually long service and excellence with a variety of awards, luncheons and parties. Many qualified, experienced Bahamians have been promoted to supervisory positions. Helpful life

Sol and Heather Kerzner.

skill seminars are held regularly to assist the employee in areas such as financial management and retirement.

Not long after his arrival in The Bahamas, Sol Kerzner announced that he would like to be a good corporate citizen and he quickly proved his intention by a $25,000 donation to the National Pride Association to beautify the environment. Sol was persuaded that the community needed more parks and green areas. He immediately promised $1.5 million for ten parks, the first being opened at Flamingo Gardens. Victims of Hurricane Floyd, underprivileged children and the Wheelchair Foundation were given relief aid by Sun International. Roots junkanoo group, Debbie Ferguson and the Golden Girls' Olympic squad all received sponsorship from Sun International. Other community projects were the Grucci fireworks display at Independence 2001 and Tourism Awareness Month highlighting ecotourism. Sun International also gave $150,000 Community Service Awards for charities approved by a panel of judges from the community leaders and Atlantis executives. Another $50,000 goes to student scholarships annually.

In March 1999, Prime Minister Hubert Ingraham opened the new $2.4 million junkanoo-coloured, dome-shaped Craft Centre, designed by Jackson Burnside. The building, situated near Hurricane Hole, features only

Bahamian made art and crafts. A new ferry terminal on the harbourside between the two bridges houses the sales desks of Dolphin Encounters and Stingray City, two popular attractions on nearby Salt Cay. Sun International also brought haute couture, exclusive fashions to the Crystal Court and Royal Towers shopping arcades. These commercial ventures have provided new opportunities for local businesses to benefit from the many visitors to Atlantis. Local boutique owner Pat Paul claims that he has done very well selling $900 suits to well-heeled tourists.[3] Atlantis also owns Logo shops in several locations throughout the Atlantis resort.

There is a very old saying, which says it pays to advertise. But it doesn't say that advertising costs a lot of money. In February 1999, Sun International launched a $20 million campaign in North America to promote Atlantis and The Bahamas as a leading resort destination. The aim was to bring in new, high-end customers and the result was that bookings were raised by 200 per cent and the brand name of Atlantis was firmly established in North America.

Sir Orville Turnquest, Governor General of The Bahamas, Sol Kerzner and HRH Prince Philip, Duke of Edinburgh at the Governor General's Award Ceremony, 1999.

The Bahamas is a jewel in a perfect setting for sporting holidays such as tennis, golf, fishing, sailing and many other water sports. Atlantis has promoted high exposure sporting events with wide media coverage. The annual Michael Jordan Celebrity Invitational and Father/Son Golf Challenge sponsored by Office Depot, attract many top golfers and celebrities and both are covered by NBC. Each year, local hero and world doubles champion, Mark Knowles, and players of the calibre of Andre Agassi support the Paradise Island Tennis Championship, which has grown year by year. The Power Boat Challenge ran for three years and was then, in 2002, replaced by the Rolex Farr 40 Sailing Championships, which brought 25 multi-millionaire owners and their entourages to the Atlantis Marina.

A constant stream of visiting celebrities gives the resort a high profile internationally. Oprah Winfrey, former South African President Nelson Mandela, former British Prime Minister Margaret Thatcher, Colin Powell, former US Presidents George Bush Senior and Jimmy Carter, Serena Williams, Rick Fox and Muhammed Ali are but a few of the starred guests who have attracted media attention. Gloria Estefan, Ricky Martin, N'Sync, Christina Aguilera, Natalie Imbruglia and other stars have filmed concerts or music videos at Paradise Island. The Disney film, 'The Voyage to Atlantis', used Atlantis sets, as did 'Holiday in the Sun' starring Mary Kate and Ashley Olsen. Television shows for MTV, E! and the Travel Channel regularly feature Paradise Island. The scenic beauty of the island was also the backdrop for the swimsuit calendar photo shoot of the Miami Dolphin cheerleaders. In late 2003, a new feature film, 'After the Sunset', starring Pierce Brosnan and Salma Hayek was shot on location at Atlantis, Paradise Island and Nassau.

In February 2001 it was announced that there was a slowdown of the economy in the USA. At first this did not affect the Paradise Island resorts, which were still registering growth. But the 11 September 2001 terrorist attack on the Pentagon and World Trade Centre had a disastrous effect on the tourist trade in The Bahamas.

For one month there was no air travel to and from the USA. Sun International's shares slumped; occupancy fell to 35 per cent compared with 68 per cent the previous September, and 1,000 staff including 150 middle managers were laid off.

The Sun International marketing team had to think quickly. They produced a poignant one-minute commercial called 'Raindrop', which showed dark clouds over New York, with a little girl looking up at the sky. A raindrop bounced up from the pavement and as it passed the girl's sad face, the image of the Royal Towers grew as the raindrop expanded to show the brightly coloured sky and sea of The Bahamas, and the little girl's face lit up with a smile. A combined N'Sync and Tim McGraw concert taped at Atlantis by CBS for Thanksgiving and radio stations from all over the country doing live remotes, as well as top entertainment television shows, kept Atlantis in the public's eye. Also in November, Atlantis hosted the Rolex Farr 40 World Sailing Championship and the sailors were very

complimentary about the weather, environment, accommodation and hospitality.

As usual the Michael Jordan and the Father/Son Golf Classic assisted in keeping the warmth of The Bahamas in the minds of the northern snowbirds. The reaction was amazing. Atlantis was booked solid for Christmas 2001, and by early February 2002 the resort was one of the first to be up to the occupancy level of the previous February. Also, many tourists who had been unable to keep their reservation in the fall, rescheduled for a later date. In February, 'Live! With Regis and Kelly' talk show aired with celebrity guests. Bahamas Weather Conference was hosted at Atlantis. More than 100 live or recorded spots from weathermen all over the country used Atlantis as a backdrop for their evening news. The Ocean Club was featured in top publications including Elle, Elite Traveler, and Departures. Innovative marketing strategies of this nature buoyed the resort through tough times.

Raindrop commercial.

On 1 July 2002, Sun International became Kerzner International, implemented in accordance with agreements related to the restructuring of the company's major shareholders.

According to rival hotelier Robert Sands, 'Atlantis stands alone almost uniquely with any hotel in the world. It is the dominant attraction in a class of its own'.[4] At the same time Paradise Island was ranked third in the world as the best Caribbean beach resort and took first place as the best family friendly beach. This honour was the latest in the long list of awards for Sol and Atlantis. Sol received a Lifetime Achievement Award from South African Hospitality and Atlantis was recognised by THEA (Themed Entertainment Association) as the best themed hotel. In addition, other awards for its excellence in the hospitality industry included: the Four Diamond Award for extraordinary service, amenities and ambiance, the Premier Recreation Award 2000 and 2001, Best Family Resort for children over 10 and Best Family Resort for children under 10.

Early predictions by Sol Kerzner indicated that Paradise Island development could stretch to seven phases, but the company had cautious optimism about Phase 3 because of the local labour environment and the threat of a resurgence of tourism in Cuba. Phase 2 was expanded to include the Ocean Club extension, the golf course, Ocean Club Estates and Harbourside Vacation Ownership Villas. Internet gambling was introduced in February 2001 and later 50 per cent was sold to a Las Vegas casino operator. It was announced in August 2001 that the Phase 3 expansion hinged on the progress of talks with Government over 'potential infrastructure improvements', including the enhancement of airport facilities and New Providence roads to transport tourists to Paradise Island. Preliminary plans were for the expansion of the marina and Phase 4 would be the development of the 55 acres at Pirate's Cove. However, there was fear of

Sol and Butch Kerzner announce the new venture 'One&Only'.

an economic slowdown in the Caribbean, which depends solely on tourism. The September 2001 terrorist attacks ran Sun into a $7.5 million quarterly loss and Phase 3 was frozen. But by December 2002, with hotels packed for the festive season, Sol announced hopes to begin Phase 3 in 2003.

Meanwhile the Kerzner group announced spending of $225 million on re-branding and expanding its luxury resorts outside The Bahamas under the new name 'One&Only'. This will include the new and improved Ocean Club alongside new hotels in Dubai, Mauritius, Mexico and the Maldives. And in January 2003, Atlantis was named 'Best Hotel in the Caribbean' by TripAdvisor.com, the leading Internet travel research engine.

After an excellent first quarter in 2003 and prolonged talks with the new Government, an agreement was reached in late May 2003 for Phase 3 to go ahead. The new expansion will comprise a new 1,200-room hotel and attractions, including a dolphin experience facility, at Pirate's Cove, Marina Village and three new luxury villas at One&Only Ocean Club, 20,000 feet of additional restaurant and retail facilities around the Atlantis Marina, 120 new vacation ownership villas at Harbourside and 50,000 feet of additional convention facilities. In a joint venture with the Government, but subject to environmental approval, a world-class, ecology sensitive, golf course will be created at the adjoining Athol Island. A fire and ambulance station will be built on Paradise Island by Kerzner International and operated by the Government. The Phase 3 project will cost $600 million and will be completed in 2007, creating 2,000 new jobs.

Sol proudly announced that Phase 3 is the most ambitious project of his 40-year career and that the development will grab world attention and the hearts and minds of every family in America. New markets will be opened up in the convention business, in the establishment of the resort as a golf destination and in the creation of a dolphin attraction for families. Kerzner International share prices soared by 20 per cent.

Paradise Island, the flagship of Kerzner International, is still the front porch of Nassau and the defining attraction that makes The Bahamas a premier destination for tourists. It will always be a 'rose' no matter what the name, be it Anne Island, Hog Island, Paradise Island or, who knows, maybe some day it will be called Atlantis.

Notes

Chapter I

1 W H Miller, 'The Colonization of the Bahamas, 1647–1670', *William and Mary Quarterly*, January 1945, p. 33

2 Ibid, p. 35

3 Ibid, p. 34

4 Mary Moseley, *The Bahamas Handbook*, (Nassau, 1926), p. 37

5 W H Miller, 'The Colonization of the Bahamas, 1647–1670', *William and Mary Quarterly*, January 1945, p. 44

6 Ibid, p. 44

7 Paul Albury, *The Story of The Bahamas*, (Macmillan, 1975), p. 49

8 Michael Craton, *A History of the Bahamas*, (Collins, 1968), p. 68

9 John Oldmixon, *The Isle of Providence*, (R H Johns Ltd, 1949), pp. 12–13

10 H E Bates, & Saunders, Hilary St George, 'The Bahamas Story', Unpublished manuscript, Bahamas House of Assembly Library, p.80

11 Calendar of State Papers, Colonial Series 11, America and West Indies 1681–1685, (Krauz Reprint Ltd, 1964), p. 579, Entry 1509

12 John Oldmixon, *The Isle of Providence*, (R H Johns Ltd, 1949), p. 13

13 *Calendar of State Papers*, Colonial Series 11, America and West Indies 1681–1685, (Krauz Reprint Ltd, 1964), p. 718, Entry 1927

14 Peter Earle, *The Wreck of the Almiranta*, (Macmillan, 1979), p. 162

Chapter 2

Except for specific notations listed below, the main source of information on Phips is Peter Earle's *The Wreck of the Almiranta*, (Macmillan, 1979). A subsidiary source is an article, 'Wrecks of Other Days', *Nassau Guardian*, 28 October 1872.

1 Michael Craton, *A History of the Bahamas*, (Collins, 1968), p. 75

2 *Calendar of State Papers*, Colonial Series 11, America and West Indies 1681–1685, (Krauz Reprint Ltd, 1964), p. 718, Entry 1927

3 Michael Craton, *A History of the Bahamas*, (Collins, 1968), p. 67

4 Mary Moseley, 'Wrecks and Wrecking in the Bahamas', *Nassau Magazine*, vol. II No.4, p. 32

Chapter 3

1 H E Bates, & Saunders, Hilary St George, 'The Bahamas Story', Unpublished manuscript, Bahamas House of Assembly Library, p.100

2 Ibid, p. 104

3 John Oldmixon, *The Isle of Providence*, (R H Johns Ltd, 1949), p. 14

4 Hareward Trott Watlinston, 'A Family Narrative'

5 Michael Craton, *A History of the Bahamas*, (Collins, 1968), p. 84

6 Paul Albury, *The Story of The Bahamas*, (Macmillan, 1975), p. 53–54

7   Mary Moseley, 'Proprietorial Government', *Nassau Guardian* (Bahamas Tercentenary Number, 1929), p. 2

8   Michael Craton, *A History of the Bahamas*, (Collins, 1968), p. 88

9   H E Bates, & Saunders, Hilary St George, 'The Bahamas Story', Unpublished manuscript, Bahamas House of Assembly Library, p. 132

10 Michael Craton, *A History of the Bahamas*, (Collins, 1968), p. 88

11 H E Bates, & Saunders, Hilary St George, 'The Bahamas Story', Unpublished manuscript, Bahamas House of Assembly Library, p. 125

12 Ibid, p. 130

13 Peter Earle, *The Wreck of the Almiranta*, (Macmillan, 1979), p. 163

14 Calendar of State Papers, Colonial Series 18, America and West Indies 1700, (Krauz Reprint Ltd, 1964), p. 256, Entry 445

15 H E Bates, & Saunders, Hilary St George, 'The Bahamas Story', Unpublished manuscript, Bahamas House of Assembly Library, p. 132

16 Ibid, p. 132

17 Ibid, p. 132

18 *Calendar of State Papers*, Colonial Series 17, America and West Indies 1699, (Krauz Reprint Ltd, 1964), p. 447, Entry 810

19 *Calendar of State Papers*, Colonial Series 19, America and West Indies 1701, (Krauz Reprint Ltd, 1964), p. 649, Entry 1042x(d)

20 *Calendar of State Papers*, Colonial Series 18, America and West Indies 1700, (Krauz Reprint Ltd, 1964), p. 136, Entry 250

21 Ibid, p. 256, Entry 445

22 *Calendar of State Papers*, Colonial Series 23, America and West Indies 1706, (Krauz Reprint Ltd, 1964), p. 115, Entry 277 II

23 H E Bates, & Saunders, Hilary St George, The Bahamas Story',Unpublished manuscript, Bahamas House of Assembly Library, p. 143

24 Henry Wilkinson, *Bermuda in the Old Empire*

Chapter 4

1   John Oldmixon, *The Isle of Providence*, (R H Johns Ltd, 1949), p. 19–20

2   H E Bates, & Saunders, Hilary St George, The Bahamas Story', Unpublished manuscript, Bahamas House of Assembly Library, p. 137

3   Ibid, p.142

4   Ibid, p. 138

5   *Calendar of State Papers*, Colonial Series 17, America and West Indies 1699, (Krauz Reprint Ltd, 1964), p. 447, Entry 810

6   H E Bates, & Saunders, Hilary St George, The Bahamas Story', Unpublished manuscript, Bahamas House of Assembly Library, p. 147

7   Ibid, p. 146

8   Michael Craton, *A History of the Bahamas*, (Collins, 1968), p. 93

9   John Oldmixon, *The Isle of Providence*, (R H Johns Ltd, 1949), pp. 22

10 Ibid, p. 18

11 H E Bates, & Saunders, Hilary St George, The Bahamas Story', Unpublished manuscript, Bahamas House of Assembly Library, p. 157

12 *Calendar of State Papers*, Colonial Series 24, America and West Indies 1708-1709, (Krauz Reprint Ltd, 1964), p. 531, Entry 870

13 Paul Albury, *The Story of The Bahamas*, (Macmillan, 1975), p. 71

14 Bryan Little, *Crusoe's Captain*, (Odham, 1960), Ch. 5

15 Ibid, p. 185

16 Paul Albury, *The Story of The Bahamas*, (Macmillan, 1975), p. 73

17 Ibid, p. 75

18 Ibid, pp. 75–76

19 Bryan Little, *Crusoe's Captain*, (Odham, 1960), p. 193

20 Ibid, p. 194

21 *Calendar of State Papers*, Colonial Series 32, America and West Indies 1720–1721, (Krauz Reprint Ltd, 1964), p. 137, Entry 224

Chapter 5

I   Paul Albury, *The Story of The Bahamas*, (Macmillan, 1975), p. 81

2   Peter Henry Bruce, *Bahamian Interlude*, (R.H. Johns Ltd, 1949), p.24

3   *Calendar of State Papers*, Colonial Series 33, America and West Indies 1722–1723, (Krauz Reprint Ltd, 1964), p. 99, Entry 207

4   C O 23/13/39 6 February 1723/4

5   C O 23/13/354 I October 1722

6   *Calendar of State Papers*, Colonial Series 34, America and West Indies 1724–1725, (Krauz Reprint Ltd, 1964), p. 131, Entry 245

7   *Proceedings of the Governor and Council, Bahamas*, (*Nassau Guardian*, Ltd, 1928), Bk. 2, p. 163

8   (i)   *War of Jenkins' Ear*
    (ii) *War of the Austrian Succession*
    (iii) *Seven Years' War*

9   H E Bates, & Saunders, Hilary St George, 'The Bahamas Story', Unpublished manuscript, Bahamas House of Assembly Library, pp. 241–242

10 C O 23/4/164 I June 1743

11 C O 23/16/152–153 October 1765

12 Paul Albury, *The Story of The Bahamas*, (Macmillan, 1975), pp. 88–89

13 Ibid, Ch. II

14 Frank H Rathbun, 'Rathbun's Raid on Nassau', *Journal of US Naval Institute* (Annapolis, Maryland) p. 46

15 Ibid, Ch. 12

16 Ibid, p. II2

17 Michael Craton, *A History of the Bahamas*, (Collins, 1968), p. 173

18 Bahamas Government Department of Lands & Surveys

Chapter 6

1   Bahamas Government Department of Lands & Surveys

2   C O 23/33/62 17 February 1794

3   Michael Craton, *A History of the Bahamas*, (Collins, 1968), p. 180

4   Ibid

5   C O 23/37/5 I November 1797

6   C O 23/37/198 8 September 1797

7   C O 23/II8/221 10 October 1844

8   *Royal Gazette*, 6 July 1822

9   Michael Craton, *A History of the Bahamas*, (Collins, 1968), p. 180

10   *Nassau Guardian*, 16 October 1852

11   *Royal Gazette*, 19 January 1831

12   *Nassau Bahamas 1823–4*, (The Bahamas Historical Society, Nassau, 1968), p. 28

13   Bahamas Government Department of Lands & Surveys

Chapter 7

1   *Nassau Guardian*, 15 August 1889, p. 1, 'Notes from the diary of an Old Bahamian'

2   R Langton-Jones, *Silent Sentinels*, (Frederick Muller Ltd., 1944), p.46

3   *Nassau Guardian*, 15 August 1889, p. 1, 'Notes from the diary of an Old Bahamian'

4   *Royal Gazette*, 12 October 1816, 'New Lighthouse', p. 2

5   *Royal Gazette*, 20 August 1817, 'Notice to Mariners'

6   C B Rawson, 'Report on the Bahamas' Hurricane of Oct. 1866', (Nassau Guardian Ltd), p. 12

7   *Nassau Guardian*, 5 November 1932, 'Thirty-seven Years as Light keeper'

8   Ibid

9   *Nassau Bahamas* 1823–4 (The Bahamas Historical Society. Nassau, 1968), p. 21

10   *Royal Gazette*, 30 July 1828

11   *Nassau Guardian*, 21 June 1939

12   R Langton-Jones, *Silent Sentinels*, (Frederick Muller Ltd, 1944)

13   Capt F W Brown, Senior Nassau Harbour Pilot, interview, 1983

14   Bahamas Government Department of Lands & Surveys

Chapter 8

1   Capt Andrew Skinner, Map of Hog Island, 1788

2   Bahamas Government Department of Lands & Surveys

3   Thelma Peterson Peters, 'The American Loyalists and the Plantation Period in the Bahama Islands', Unpublished thesis, the University of Florida, 1960, p. 81

4   Ibid

5   *Bahama Gazette*, 20 May 1791

6   *Bahama Gazette*, 14 June 1791

7   *Royal Gazette*, 11 February 1829

8   C O 23/189/429 Rawson's Report, 1867

9   *Nassau Guardian*, 18 December 1872 and 9 June 1875

10   *Nassau Guardian*, 27 June 1897

11   *Nassau Guardian*, 8 October 1864

12   *Nassau Guardian*, 9 June 1875

13   *Nassau Guardian*, 7 March 1874

14   *Nassau Guardian*, 19 June 1889

15 *Nassau Guardian*, 23 November 1901

16 Ibid

17 *Nassau Guardian*, 12 December 1903

18 *Nassau Guardian*, 12 August 1905

19 *Nassau Guardian*, 24 August 1907

20 *Nassau Guardian*, 14 June 1924

21 Berdelle Key, former employee of the West India Oil Company, interview, 1982

22 *Nassau Guardian*, 14 June 1924

23 *The Tribune*, 23 April 1924

24 *The Tribune*, 2 August 1924

25 *Nassau Guardian*, 14 June 1924

26 Mary Moseley, *Nassau Guardian* (Centenary Number) November 1944

27 *Nassau Guardian*, 14 June 1924

Chapter 9

1 C O 23/189/429 Rawson's Report, 1867

2 *Nassau Guardian*, 8 July 1871

3 Paul Albury, *The Story of the Bahamas*, (Macmillan, 1975), p. 166

4 William Benedict Reilly, 'The Bahamas', *Monthly Illustrator*, vol. XIII, No.4, November 1896, p. 15

5 Ibid

6 *Nassau Guardian*, 6 October 1923

7 *Nassau Guardian*, 15 August 1908

8 *Nassau Guardian*, 27 January 1897

9 Ibid

10 *Nassau Guardian*, 22 January 1898

11 *Nassau Guardian*, 15 September 1900

12 *Nassau Guardian*, 13 January 1900

13 Ibid

14 Ibid

15 *Nassau Guardian*, March 1900

16 *Nassau Guardian*, 8 January 1910

17 Michael Craton, *A History of the Bahamas*, (Collins, 1968), p. 259

18 Mary Moseley, *The Bahamas Handbook*, (Nassau Guardian Ltd 1926), p. 154

19 Ibid

20 Charles Hall, former Munson employee. Interview 1982

21 Ibid

22 Mary Mosely, *Nassau Guardian* (Centenary Number) 1944

23 Charles Hall, former Munson employee. Interview 1982

24 Ibid

Chapter 10

Except for specific notations listed below, the main source of information for Club Mediterranée was Mr Barry Scott, and for the Yoga Retreat Ms Rhoda Ireland.

1   *Nassau Guardian*, 25 January 1930

2   *Nassau Guardian*, 23 December 1931

3   *Nassau Guardian*, 8 February 1930

4   Ibid

5   Ibid

6   Ibid

7   Capt F W Brown, Senior Nassau Harbour Pilot, interview, 1983

Chapter 11

1   Winston S Churchill, *The Gathering Storm*, (Houghton Mifflin Co., 1948), p. 423

2   John Dahllof, crew member of the *Southern Cross*, interview, 1982

3   Winston S Churchill, *The Gathering Storm*, (Houghton Mifflin Co., 1948), p. 423

4   *Nassau Guardian*, 20 March 1939

5   Ibid

6   *Nassau Guardian*, 18 March 1939

7   *Nassau Guardian*, 20 April 1939

8   *Nassau Guardian*, 12 April 1939

9   *Nassau Guardian*, 23 May 1938

10 John Dahllof, crew member of the *Southern Cross*, and his wife, former employee of Wenner-Gren, interview, 1982

11 Ibid

12 Ibid

13 Ibid

14 Geoffrey A D Johnstone, lawyer, interview, 1982

15 John Dahllof, crew member of the *Southern Cross*, interview, 1982

16 *Bahamas Handbook and Businessman's Annual*, 4th edn, (Etienne Dupuch, Jr. Pub., 1964), p. 331

Chapter 12

1   Geoffrey A D Johnstone, lawyer, interview, 1982

2   *Herald Tribune* (New York) 23 February 1964, 'The Luther of Columbus Circle' by Tom Wolfe, p. 14

3   Ibid, p. 13

4   Ibid

5   Geoffrey A D Johnstone, lawyer, interview, 1982

6   *Bahamas Handbook and Businessman's Annual*, 3rd edn, (Etienne Dupuch, Jr. Pub., 1963), p. 96

7   Roy MacKeen, manager of Nassau Shipyards Ltd, interview, 1983

8   Ibid

9   Geoffrey A D Johnstone, lawyer, interview, 1982

10 Material supplied by Mr Barrie Farrington, Executive Vice President of Resorts International (Bahamas) Ltd

11 Ibid

12 Ibid

13 Geoffrey A D Johnstone, lawyer, interview, 1982

14 *The Tribune*, 15 November 1963

15 Roy MacKeen, manager of Nassau Shipyards Ltd, interview, 1983

16 Ibid

17 Geoffrey A D Johnstone, lawyer, interview, 1982

Chapter 13

Except for the specific notations listed below, the main source of information on Resorts International was supplied by Mr Barrie Farrington, Executive Vice-President of Resorts International (Bahamas) Ltd

1 Paul Albury, *The Story of The Bahamas*, (Macmillan, 1975), p. 258

2 *Bahamas Handbook and Businessman's Annual*, 6th edn, (Etienne Dupuch, Jr. Pub., 1966), p. 263

3 *The Tribune*, 16 March 1966

4 *Bahamas Handbook and Businessman's Annual*, 6th edn, (Etienne Dupuch, Jr. Pub., 1966), p. 266

5 *The Tribune*, 4 December 1972

6 *Nassau Guardian*, 16 August 1973

7 *The Tribune*, 17 October 1974

8 *The Tribune*, 25 August 1976

9 *The Tribune*, 28 November 1973

10 *Nassau Guardian*, 30 November 1981

11 *Nassau Guardian*, 20 March 1939

Chapter 14

1 *The Tribune*, 20th May 1983

Chapter 16

1 *The Tribune*, 7th May 1992

2 *The Tribune*, 3rd January 1995

3 *The Tribune*, 3rd April 1997

Chapter 17

1 Interview with Sol Kerzner, 28th October 2002

2 All quotations except those noted separately are from A G Galanopoulos and Edward Bacon, *Atlantis: The Truth behind the Legend*, Appendix A: Extract Critias by Plato 115C, (Bobbs-Merrill Co. 1969), pp. 179–191

3 Interview with Pat Paul, June 2002

4 *The Tribune*, 28th November 2002

Index